St. Augustine's First Footfall

An investigation into the probable location of the landing site of Augustine's mission in 597AD

Gerald Moody

2013

First published 2013

Trust for Thanet Archaeology
The Antoinette Centre, Quex Park,
Birchington, Kent, CT7 0BH
www.thanetarch.co.uk

ISBN 978 0 9576512 1 0

Typesetting and origination by Trust for Thanet Archaeology

Printed by Bonacia Ltd. UK

CONTENTS

APPENDIX

LIST OF FIGURES

LIST OF PLATES

THE REASON FOR REVIEWING THE LANDING SITE

The Trust for Thanet Archaeology has been at the forefront of research in the local history of the Isle of Thanet for 25 years. The leading characters who formed the Trust met at the excavation of the Bronze Age burial mounds and Anglo-Saxon cemetery at Ozengell, Ramsgate in the mid 1970's. The view from the site encompassed the Wantsum river valley and Pegwell Bay, with Richborough in the background, the very area into which in 597, Augustine would have sailed.

In Augustine's time, the Wantsum river divided the Isle of Thanet from mainland Kent. Much has been written and speculated from that time, but it is only since the work carried out by Ges Moody on the historic sea levels and the dynamics of coastal change, along with recent archaeological work on the Wantsum valley, that a better understanding of the possible landing site has become possible.

I have commissioned this study so that readers can visualise St. Augustine's passage across the bay below St. Augustine's church toward the wide Pegwell Bay and the entrance to the Stour and the valley of the Wantsum. My personal thanks go to Ges Moody and his colleagues for this investigation into the most likely landing site.

David Steed

Founder Chairman of the Trust for Thanet Archaeology and Friend of St. Augustine's Church

FOREWORD

Interest in the figure of St Augustine is on the rise. And so it should be. The subject of Augustine's landing is of national significance. The saint's arrival began the Christian history of the Anglo-Saxon people which in turn has brought forth so many cultural and religious treasures for humanity.

Following the popular 1997 celebrations of the 1400th anniversary of the Augustine mission and after last year's institution on a new official shrine of St Augustine in Pugin's personal church in Ramsgate, it is opportune to revisit the much debated question of the precise place and circumstances of the saint's arrival in 597 AD.

Many investigators in more recent times had doubted the original account, given by the Venerable Bede, that St Augustine came to the Isle of Thanet. Now, however, with new research into the geography of the 6th century east Kent coastline along with a fresh evaluation of the existing evidence in light of better awareness of the cultural conditions of the place and period, this re-appraisal of the traditional account has been made possible.

I'm delighted to commend this work and hope that its important subject matter receives a wide readership and deserved appreciation.

Fr. Marcus Holden M.A. (Oxon.), S.T.L.

Parish Priest of Ramsgate and Minster and Custodian of the Shrine of St Augustine

20th April 2013

ACKNOWLEDGEMENTS

I would like to thank David and Edwina Steed for commissioning this investigation into the possible sites of the landing place of St. Augustine and for their encouragement and enthusiasm for the project during the period of its production. The time taken to write and illustrate the book extended considerably from the original estimate as both my interest in the subject matter, and my narration of it, grew in complexity and depth. I would also like to extend my thanks to Emma Boast for her skills in illustration and production which have helped immeasurably in the process of bringing this book to print. I would also like to thank my colleague at the Trust for Thanet Archaeology, Adam Webber for assisting with the reproduction of some of the images and his work on some of the illustrations. Thanks are also due to Ludmilla Onuferova for permission to use the original photographic images of the stained glass window depicting St. Augustine taken in the church and the picture of the church reproduced at the end of the book. I would also like to thank Edwina Steed for the original artwork which forms the basis of the design for the cover of the book.

Gerald Moody April 2013

PREFACE

The mission of Augustine, a monk sent by Pope Gregory the Great from a monastery in Rome to bring Christianity to the Anglo-Saxon kingdoms of the Island of Britain, shaped the character of the culture and history of the country for the next millennium.

In the two centuries before Augustine set out, the provinces of Europe which were once part of the Western Roman Empire had separated into regional kingdoms, ruled by men whose cultural traditions were both Roman and Germanic in origin. While the Roman Empire adopted Christianity as an official state religion under Constantine I in the 4th century AD, many of the new European rulers had adopted the Arian form of Christianity before they had entered the Empire. Others, like the people from northern Germany who settled the east coast of Britain, still adhered to one of the many local and regional forms of religious worship, of idols or aspects of the natural world, which were characterised as Pagan.

It was through the introduction of the Roman Church to Britain by Augustine that the country was able to join the common culture that emerged from the ruins of the Roman Empire. The establishment of the Christian religion, as it was practised in Rome, supplanting paganism and several unorthodox sects, became a defining element of European history in the middle ages.

Historical sources place the first landing in Britain of Augustine and his company of monks, on the Isle of Thanet, at the eastern limit of Kent, in 597 AD. It was here that Augustine's first meeting with King Aethelbert, who ruled in Kent from around 560 AD until his death in 616, probably took place. The landing took place in a maritime landscape, which had undoubtedly played a significant role in the narrative of both the earlier Roman occupation of Britain and in the arrival of new invaders and settlers who transformed Romano-British culture from the early 5th century.

Gaps in the narrative offered by the historical sources, giving few details of the circumstances of Augustine's arrival, have stimulated a tradition of historical geography which has tried to locate the events within the regional landscape. Additional evidence for the context to the arrival of

12

Augustine has been added by the development of archaeology as a discipline from the middle of the 19th century, which has stimulated the progressive revision of ideas about the historical significance of the event.

In the absence of a recent summary of the evidence of the physical context of Augustine's arrival, this work examines new evidence for the character of the landscape and reviews new appreciations of the cultural conditions prevailing in the later 6th century. The work reconsiders, not just the issue of where Augustine had the opportunity to land, but also where it may have been proper for him to land, taking into account his own status, his mission and the character of the people he was sent to convert.

INTRODUCTION

Space is limited in a short work such as this to undertake a detailed historiographical examination of the many secondary historical works that give accounts of Augustine's arrival in Britain and, more specifically, deal with the actual landing place of his party.

In 1949 Harold Bing published a useful summary list of all the sources and secondary literature produced to that date[1]. The main works were identified as the letters of Pope Gregory the Great concerning the mission of Augustine; Bede's account in his Ecclesiastical History of the English People; a series of works produced by churchmen including a life of Augustine produced by Goscelin and a series of chronicles produced by monks of St. Augustine's Abbey at Canterbury; Thomas Sprott (whose work is lost but reproduced in part by Thorne), William Thorne and Thomas of Elmham. Also listed were a series of secondary historical considerations produced in the 19th century, notably the text of a lecture titled the Landing of Augustine and the Conversion of Ethelbert, given by Dean Arthur Stanley at Canterbury on April 28th 1854[2]. In 1897 a handbook containing the relevant primary documents of the Mission of St Augustine to England was compiled by Canon A.J. Mason and published by the Cambridge University Press[3]. More recent works, produced in a modern historiographical tradition, beginning with Henry Howarth's book Augustine of Canterbury[4], generally explore the wider perspective of the early Church or the Anglo-Saxon period in general and are not concerned with the micro history of Augustine's arrival and landing place, moving on quickly from the issue after a brief restatement of a narrative that follows one of the earlier secondary sources.

Mason's preface established that, in the matter of Augustine's mission, only two sources were sufficiently authentic to preserve all that is authentically known in a single volume, the letters written by Pope Gregory the Great and Bede's account [5]. Mason concluded that it was *scarcely worthwhile to refer to later authorities* such Goscelin's Life, or the works of Canterbury chroniclers as they have *no historical information to impart*, relying ultimately on Bede's account, or secondary works for their narrative.

In this body of secondary works, where the authors retell the narrative for their own times and purposes, little reliable historical or geographical detail is imparted which can be used for the purpose of this work. Other than Bede, the secondary sources are mainly useful for exploring how the story of Augustine has been interpreted and embellished over time. In summary, the only primary sources that are available for Augustine's mission remain Gregory's letters. Bede's narrative is our most valuable secondary source, without which we would have no data at all on Augustine's arrival in England.

Bede's Ecclesiastical History[6] was compiled in 731 AD from a range of documents and accounts principally supplied to him by Albinus, Abbott of St. Augustine's Abbey[7]. The text includes reasonably accurate reproductions of Gregory's letters, although there are some minor errors of transcription. Bede had an awareness of the responsibilities of a historian and in his text distinguished between authoritative sources and less reliable testimony[8]. We must rely on Bede's integrity as a historian and assume his narrative is founded on authentic details.

We are not given by Bede's account, written in 731 AD, any of the fine detail of the circumstances of Augustine's landing. With the phrase *'On this island landed the servant of the Lord, Augustine, and his companions'*[9], the point of disembarkation is given as being in Thanet, without naming a particular spot or adding any descriptive detail. From neither the primary, or the best of our secondary sources, are we able to extract enough information to definitively place the site in the modern or ancient landscape.

There are many reasons for wanting to understand more about the circumstances of Augustine's first days in Britain. For the believer, there is a reverence for one of the primary locations in the history of the foundation of the Roman Catholic Church in Britain. To the historian of cultures, there is an interest in the impact of Augustine's arrival on the prevailing customs and mentality of an emerging society, which was suddenly reconnected with a wider world which had, briefly forgotten it. Both interests have been expressed through examining the geography of Augustine's first days in Britain, where the physical circumstances of the narrative have been used to explore the cultural impact. These approaches emerged from two separate historiographical traditions, the narration of the origins of Christianity and the works of its significant characters, which is represented in the chronicles written by monks at Augustine's own abbey; and the study of the historical geography of Kent, which developed in the Tudor renaissance in the writing of Leland, Twyne, Lambard and Stukeley, who all attempted to trace wider aspects of Kent's history in the physical landscape [10].

Writers who have considered the circumstances of Augustine's arrival in detail have made a case for one site or another as the actual place of landing and attempted to identify the locations of the subsequent events of Augustine's first days in Britain. Although unnamed in our most authoritative sources, places like Ebbsfleet, Richborough and Stonar, have been bound to the narrative. The origin and navigability of the Wantsum River, which Bede described as dividing Thanet from the mainland of Kent[11], has also figured in the discussions. At best the analysis has been made on the basis of direct observation of the landscape, at worst from repetition of assertions by secondary authorities, obscured by misinformation or from poor reasoning. The evaluation of these ideas is complicated by recent changes in the landscape of the southern side of Thanet and the eastern part of the Wantsum, caused by natural and human actions, which now make it difficult to reconsider many of the potential locations by direct observation.

Our understanding of the cultural context of the meeting between Augustine and Aethelbert has changed over time, as we have gained a better understanding of the historical and archaeological evidence for the environment in which it took place. More is known about the complexity of the 'Anglo-Saxon' culture which Augustine's mission was directed to convert to Roman Catholicism, and of the emerging European nations that succeeded the Roman Empire. Until recently, interpretations of the early Anglo-Saxon kingdoms were tinged with the nostalgia for the lost classical world which pervaded the British education system over the past five hundred years[12]. Interpretations were also influenced by Britain's experience as an imperial power from the 16th to the mid 20th century. For example, reflecting contemporary views of first contacts between cultures, a footnote to Stanley's narrative of Augustine's meeting with Aethelbert, casts the encounter as one recognisable in any remote colonial outpost: *'Exchange English travellers for Roman missionaries, Arab sheiks for Saxon chiefs... [to] give us some notion of this celebrated dialogue'* [13]. In many accounts there is a sense that, as one writer put it, Britain had been *'swallowed up in the darkness of the north'*, and that Augustine's Mission was entering the heart of that darkness [14].

With the perspective of the 160 years of historical and archaeological research that has been carried out in the region, the character and background of the agents in the narrative can be filled out with much greater detail and sophistication. In his review of the subject in 1949, Bing questioned whether the prevailing view of the barbarian character of the Jutes was a fair representation of the historical people, and of Aethelbert their King who had after all, married Bertha, the Christian daughter of a Frankish King[15]. Much of the evidence for the contemporary population, who are lost to the written record, has been added by the discovery and analysis of the remains of their bodies, clothes and possessions through archaeological research[16].

We have a greater appreciation of the longevity of some of the sites within the landscape in question, and a more detailed knowledge of the role they played in the history of the Roman Empire, which had only recently diminished as a power in the country. More is known now about the physical geography of the region, allowing a better reconstruction of the spatial circumstances of Augustine's arrival to be carried out[17].

For the foregoing reasons a re-examination of the geographical and cultural context of the landing place of Augustine remains a significant matter for enquiry, for this work and other works drawn on, or referenced within it.

INTERPRETATIONS OF THE LANDING PLACE

No details of Augustine's route from mainland Europe to Thanet are given by any of the sources, nor are details of the passage given. The only evidence for the route taken are the letters supplied by Pope Gregory, addressed to the Bishops of several cities in Gaul, Lyons, Arles, Aix and Lerin, and to Arigius, the patrician of Gaul. He also addressed letters to the Frankish Kings, brothers Theoderic and Theudebert and their grandmother Brunhilda[1]. It is not clear whether Augustine passed through all these cities and regions or whether the letters were prepared in case they were needed according to the route he chose. The party, now according to Bede numbering as many as 40 people, made the crossing of the Dover Strait from one of the ports on the north east coast of Gaul. One likely point of departure is the port of Quentovic in the Canche valley south of Boulogne, which was the principal port for the Frankish Kingdoms and became an important route of pilgrimage from Anglo-Saxon England to Rome[2].

It has been suggested that if the monks and the people they took with them, travelled together in a large ship, they might have had to take part in the rowing themselves[3]. It is not obvious that Augustine's party would have been suited to, or qualified for the task, and if they were taken as passengers in a single ship, it must have been a substantial vessel, perhaps determining the choice of landing place.

The only useful source that can be used to reconstruct any chronological or geographical detail of Augustine's landing, is Bede's account (Appendix 1) which specifically states that Augustine came ashore on Thanet (Figure 1 shows all the location in Thanet that are mentioned in the following text). Bede describes Thanet briefly in the preceding passages, noting its occupation by 600 families, to give an idea of the relatively large scale of the island in contrast to other smaller inhabited islands, and notes that it was separated from the mainland of Kent by what he calls the Wantsum river (*fluuius Uantsumu*)[4].

Bing pointed out that the Canterbury chroniclers were consistent in placing the landing site at Richborough (Fig. 1, **A**), however there is confusion over whether this was intended to mean directly at the site

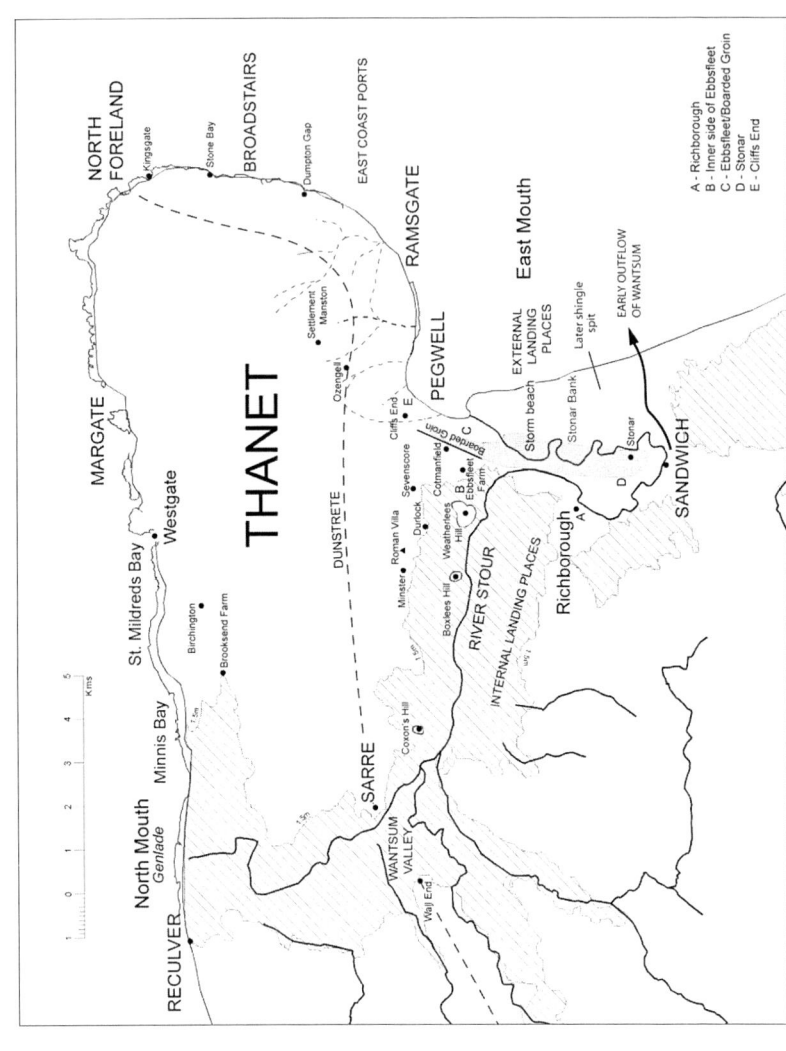

Figure 1. Map of the Isle of Thanet showing the location of sites and places mentioned in the text.

where the remains of a Roman fort and town are located, or if the name is used as it was in Roman times as a general term for the region, encompassing several potential landing places, reopening the question of on exactly which spot the landing took place.

In a footnote at the end of his published lecture Dean Arthur Stanley listed the four probable landing spots identified by previous writers and the main arguments for and against them[5]. The first was Ebbsfleet, because local historical tradition, including Thanet's 18th century historian John Lewis (and by Edward Hasted reproducing Lewis), has favoured locating Augustine's landing at 'Ebbsfleet' because it was the *'usual landing place'* in Thanet. The evidence given for this is the Anglo-Saxon chronicle from the place named as the landing place of Hengist, an early Saxon mercenary who reputedly founded a Kingdom in Kent. However, there is a great deal of variation in the spelling of the place name in the texts of the different versions of the Chronicle and there is no direct evidence to associate the name to the present site of Ebbsfleet Farm (Fig. 1, **B**) or to the Ebbsfleet peninsula on the southern side of Thanet and eventually the association with any actual location has become a tautology[6].

The second location identified by Stanley was an area on the eastern side of Thanet known as the Boarded Groin, where in the 18th century a sea wall protected the eastern side of the Ebbsfleet peninsula from erosion by the sea (Fig. 1, **C**). The two further sites identified were Stonar, at the southern end of a shingle spit extending from Thanet and Richborough (Fig. 1, **D**), both of which Stanley rejected because they are not on Thanet, and are therefore in contradiction to Bede's narrative.

Rejecting the historical authority of the place which now bears the name of Ebbsfleet as the landing site does not rule out the possibility that some of the locations that have been associated with it are candidates in the search for Augustine's landing place. In his history of the Isle of Thanet published in 1739, John Lewis wrote

> *'Just at the mouth of the Richborough Port is Ebbisfleet a little creek or bay where vessels used to harbour, and where was the usual landing-*

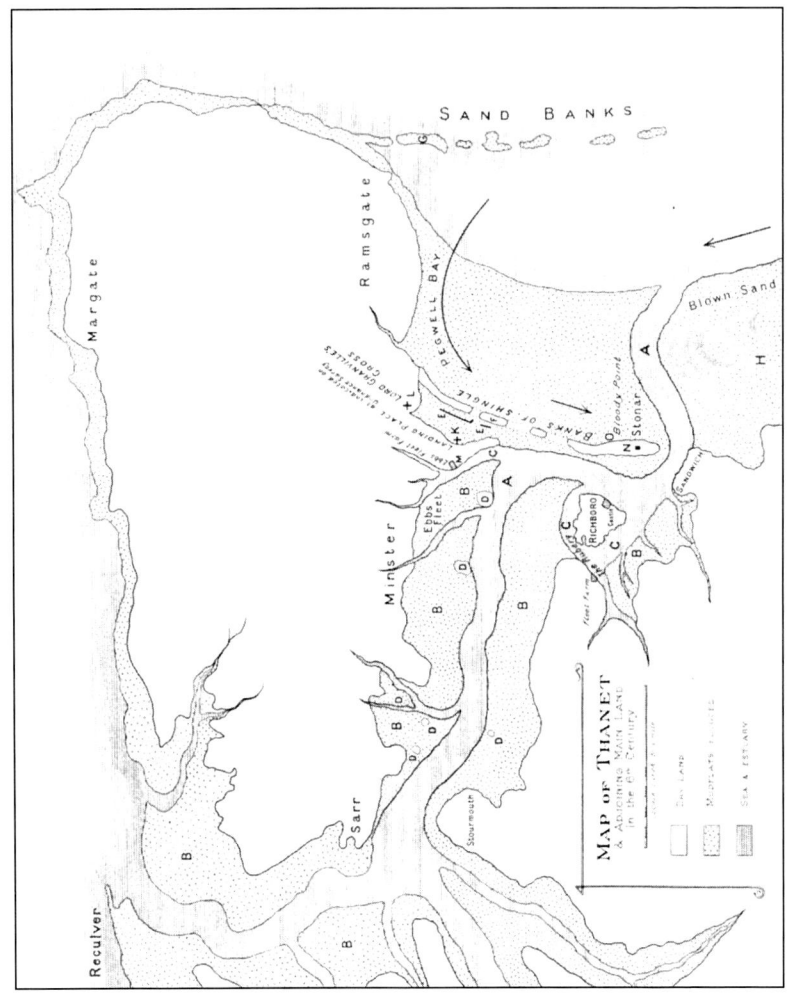

Figure 2. McKenny-Hughes' map of Thanet in the 6th century AD published in 1897.

place in this island from the ocean...[here] did Hengist and Horsa land...[and] here Austin the Monk came on shore.'

Lewis located Ebbsfleet to the east of the houses of Ebbsfleet farm, on the seaward side of the peninsula near the Boarded Groin, near a field called Cotmanfeld. Stanley had rejected this site because *'it must have been covered by the sea'*, however his own work uses Lewis as an authority for the location of the landing at Ebbsfleet. Conditions at the location may have been quite different in the past before the coastal erosion that provoked the construction of the Boarded Groin had progressed so far.

In the late 19th century an attempt was made to carry out a more scientific assessment of the landscape context, to be able to place the story in a more convincing setting. Two significant considerations of the geological and geographic evidence for the location of Augustine's first landing have been carried out by T. McKenny Hughes, Woodwardian Professor of Geology at the University of Cambridge, to accompany Mason's handbook in 1897[7]; and one by local geologist George Dowker, published in *Archaeologia Cantiana* also in 1897[8]. Both articles included maps of the floodplain of the River Stour and the Wantsum to support their arguments. McKenny Hughes's map is a reconstruction of the coast in the 6th century (Fig. 2); Dowker's map (Fig. 3) showed the present condition of the landscape.

Dowker struggled with a theme that persisted in contemporary works, which suggested that the Wantsum had once been open to the sea at the eastern end from Cliffsend to Deal. His observation that a map, published posthumously to accompany John Battely's book *Antiquitates Rutupinae* (Antiquities of Richborough; Figure 4), took little account of the actual topography of the area and so had grossly exaggerated the area of open water between the Isle of Thanet and the mainland, is particularly significant to the historiography of the Wantsum, explaining the origin of this tradition. Hughes and Dowker agreed that, rather than an open channel, a central channel was intersected by minor watercourses, or fleets, extending from springs emanating from the minor valleys that flanked the main watercourse. Dowker traced historical documents that referred to a smaller river channel or fleet,

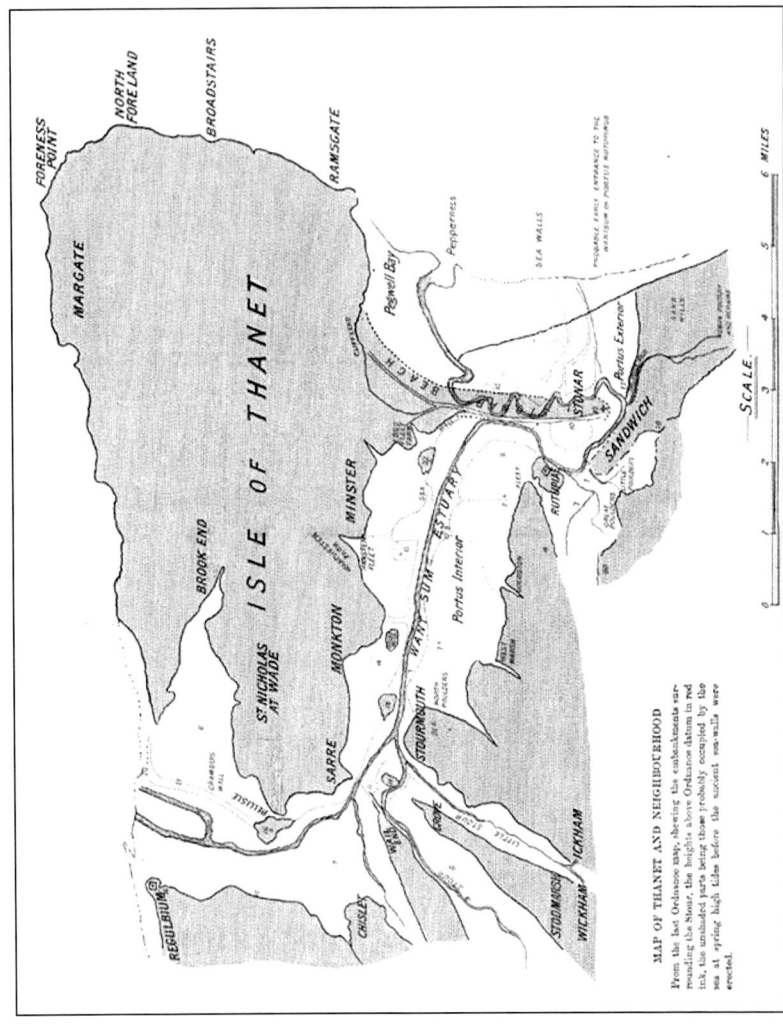

MAP OF THANET AND NEIGHBOURHOOD

From the last Ordnance map, shewing the embankments surrounding the Stour, the heights above Ordnance datum in red ink, the unshaded parts being those probably occupied by the sea at spring high tides before the nearest sea-walls were erected.

Figure 3. George Dowker's map of Thanet and neighbourhood published in 1897.

23

extending from the western side of the Ebbsfleet peninsula, past Durlock and as far as Minster. The map drawn by McKenny Hughes also reconstructs fleets extending from the main channel to Minster and the western side of the Ebbsfleet peninsula, at Sevenscore and Durlock. A navigable fleet reaching as far as Minster has important implications because of the recent discovery of a large Roman Villa on the slopes to the east of the spring, which flows out of the Wantsum valley at that location[9].

Both authors recognised that a very significant feature in the Wantsum landscape was a beach, extending from north to south from Cliffsend to Stonar, which had undoubtedly been dry land and had been occupied in the Roman period. They agreed that the beach originated at an early period; it was certainly pre-Roman and was possibly of prehistoric date; and had once extended across the eastern entrance to the Wantsum valley, screening it from the full force of the open sea and creating two distinct regions, one on the east side of the beach, external to the valley, and one west of the beach internal to the valley. They also drew attention to a second shingle spit of more recent origin, progressing steadily from south to north, which was gradually occluding the original opening to the interior region which was located at the southern terminal of the earlier beach.

Dowker's analysis of the misleading map provide a substantial clarification of the geography of the eastern mouth of the Wantsum, putting the locations identified in earlier works and new ideas into a much more accurate context. To Stanley's original list of possible landing sites McKenny Hughes added the western side of the Ebbsfleet peninsula, on the interior of the Wantsum valley on one of the smaller fleets, on the opposite side of the peninsula to the location identified by Lewis.

Dowker argued that the western bank of Stonar, on the interior of the Wantsum valley would have been a suitable candidate for the landing place, allowing Augustine's party to wait before crossing the lagoon and being admitted to Richborough to meet with the King. However, Stonar had been rejected by Stanley because he thought it must only have been

Figure 4. Map of Rutupian Ports published with Battely's Antiquities of Richborough.

a large island at the time and it was not in Thanet, so contradicting Bede's evidence. Generally the possible locations given for a landing in the historical works that have subjected the issue to analysis have been chosen on the basis of two elements, firstly the landscape context and secondly ideas about how the political and cultural roles of the agents involved shaped their movements in that landscape. Each author has created a conceptual 'political geography', reflecting their current knowledge of the historical and landscape context, which was substituted for any further clues from the historical sources.

McKenny Hughes actually came down in favour of a direct landing on the raised island at Richborough, on the general authority of the Canterbury chronicles, and on the assumption that it would have been deserted[10]. He imagined the monks sheltering in the ruined walls of the fortress, isolated from the main land arguing that Aethelbert may have felt that putting water between them would act as a sort of *spiritual disinfectant*' until the meeting could take place in the open outside the fort.

It is clear that all the arguments for a landing place, given in the secondary historical works, have been based on an outdated understanding of the cultural context and the theme of the location of Augustine's landing needs to be re-examined. For example, the choice of the site of the Roman Fort and town at Richborough by many of the 19th century authors is based on an anachronistic view of the history of that area, which has been undermined by archaeological investigations at the fortress carried out in the early 20th century[11]. For example McKenny Hughes argued that no Roman Road was to be found at Richborough, nor evidence for Anglo-Saxon occupation at the site. Both these points have since been disproved, a Roman road has now been found, along with a marble clad monument, which represented a gateway to Britain and stood briefly on the road at the centre of the forts and Roman town; coins, burials and other evidence of Anglo-Saxon settlement have also been recovered. If as McKenny Hughes argued, the port at Richborough held a similar importance to the Saxons as it had the Romans, it seems to have been defended and maintained using the same walls which remained from the Roman fort and was far from deserted.

Revisiting the Landscape

The foregoing review of the opinions of previous writers on the historic landing place of Augustine has identified some of the main geological and geographical factors involved in identifying potential sites. It will be helpful to review the current evidence for the following elements; the geological origin and potential navigability of the Wantsum river; the origin and dynamics of the earlier shingle beach between Stonar and Pegwell and of the later shingle spit growing northwards from Deal, their effect on the navigability of the channel and influence on the choice of landing places on the east side of the coast; and finally the historic effect of extreme weather events on the region, their influence on the long term stability of the flow of the river and tides through the Wantsum and the implications for the historic navigability of the river.

A revised reconstruction of the landscape contemporary with Augustine's arrival must take into account a wide range of sources. McKenny Hughes and Dowker together gave a concise assessment of the conditions prevailing in the Wantsum valley in the later 19th century[1] and further detail was added to the general geological background to the area by the publication in 1928 of the memoirs of the Geological Survey covering the area near Ramsgate and Dover[2]. In addition the first edition of the one inch Ordnance Survey, surveyed between 1791 and 1810 and published in 1819, preserves a model of the area before the landscape was altered forever in the later 19th and early 20th century, by the construction of the railway in 1847, new wharfs on the Stour in the early 20th century and the installation of a military supply base in 1916. Much of the relevant areas of the landscape described in these documentary sources can no longer be fully appreciated by inspection on the ground and they are invaluable for the reconstruction of the 6th century landscape.

New sources of information are now available, Earth sciences have made rapid progress in the last two centuries and to present any new interpretation of the possible landing place of Augustine's mission, the geographical context needs to be viewed with the benefit of the most recent tools. With the power of sophisticated measuring devices that

5.1 Elevation model generated from SRTM data

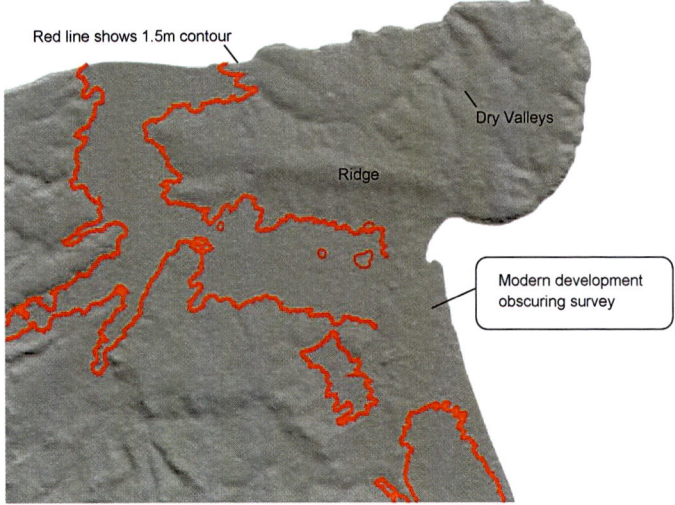

5.2 First edition One Inch Ordnance Survey 1819 with contour lines overlaid

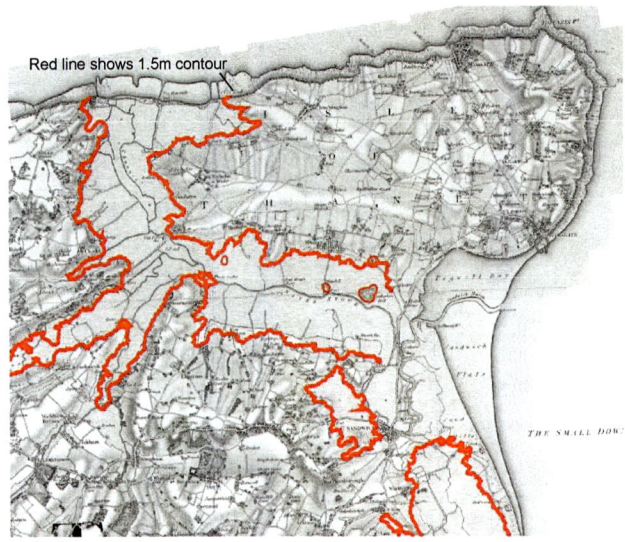

Figure 5. Reconstructions of the alluvial plain of the Wantsum.

record in fine detail the surface of the earth and the sea bed, combined with modern computer modelling of the detail of the landscape, we can add more than ever before to the story of the landscape to reconstruct the prevailing conditions at Augustine's arrival. It is possible to verify Dowker and McKenny-Hughes's observations using the first edition of the Ordnance Survey, alongside the additional evidence from archaeology or additional data from remote sensing methods[3].

The Wantsum

As Dowker noted, previous attempts to reconstruct the limits of the Wantsum by tracing from a contour at too high an elevation, or by extending the dimensions of the channel to the limits of the alluvial plain from a map run the risk of exaggerating the historic dimensions of the channel. In his narrative Bede described the Wantsum 'river' as being 3 stadia wide, conventionally translated as 3 furlongs, in the region of 600m[4]. This simple characterisation does not adequately describe the dimensions of the alluvial plain that can be observed from an elevation model of the valley, generated with the aid of fine measurements of elevations sampled by an instrument aboard the NASA Space Shuttle (Shuttle Radar Tomography Mission; Fig. 5.1). The outer limits of the plain can be traced from the boundary with the steeper slopes of the main land mass by generating very fine contours from the elevation data; the first consistent contour at the outer limit of the plain stands at an elevation of 1.5 metres above Ordnance Datum.

When the two independently measured coverages of the elevation model and the First Edition of the one inch Ordnance Survey are overlaid, this 1.5m contour boundary conforms well with limits to the alluvial marshes that are depicted on the map (Fig. 5.2). Because of the low resolution of the radar tomography survey which can not detect the minor changes to the marsh edges that have taken place since the survey in 1819, the map provides more accurate information for some of the finer local details, particularly of the inlets shown at Durlock and the limits of the Marshes on the west of the Boarded Groin. This demonstrates that a detailed study of this first Ordnance Survey map, a historical document of immense accuracy and value, will give as close an account as possible of the outer limit of the alluvial basin of the Wantsum, before the changes in the 20th century associated with the construction of a military port and supply depot in the First World War at Stonar.

Archaeological discoveries within the boundaries of the Wantsum valley also give an indication of the historical limits of the reach of water in the channel. Bronze Age monuments have been exposed on the lower reaches of the southern tip of the Ebbsfleet peninsula and a Roman cremation and foundations were found on Boxlees Hill, and burial urns are recorded at Weatherlees Hill, both of which stood as islands of un-eroded geological deposits from the base of the valley, standing between water courses which have cut their way around these features[5]. A Roman building was exposed when a railway line was constructed at the foot of the scarp below Richborough fort, not far above the upper range of the Stour's tidal range in the present day[6]. It is therefore unlikely that the normal reach of the Wantsum ever exceeded the limits of the alluvial plane that has been established by this analysis of the data. Further evidence for the shape and extent of the Wantsum must be sought in its geological origins.

Geological origin of the Wantsum

The alluvium that settled in the channel masks a landform with a very long history (Fig. 6.1). Recent research suggests that formation of the Dover strait, which forms the eastern limit of the valley separating Thanet from the mainland of Kent, took place around a quarter of a million years ago during the glacial maximums in the current Pleistocene Glaciation[7]. The mass of land that would form Kent was a bulging dome of rock, flanked by the sloping chalk faces of the South and North Downs. A continuous ridge linked what are now the North Downs to the chalk geology of northern France. A section of the North Downs chalk was separated from the main mass by an ancient tectonic fold, which formed a dip and an east to west ridge, which crosses what is now the Isle of Thanet. In a so called 'Mega Flood' event, a lake that had formed at the head of the advancing ice sheets against the north eastern face of the ridge, spilled over the chalk ridge, gouging braided channels through the rock as billions of gallons of water flowed out, truncating the eastern end of the fold.

At the end of the last Ice Age, around 10,000 years ago, sea levels stood some 130m below their present level. The combined flows of the great Thames and the Rhine flowed westward through the channels in the Dover Strait gap, as a combined Channel river, to reach the sea some distance west of the coast of Britain today. To the west of the junction where the folded dip and ridge met, a deep channel carrying the drainage from the chalk slope of the North Downs and the springs that flowed from valleys that flanked it, was scoured through the north facing slope of chalk through the southern bank of the valley of the Thames. The north south orientated valley and the east west orientated folded dip, intersected at a right angle at the western end of the central ridge. A regular series of minor valleys flanked the dip and the combined flows of springs emanating from the valleys traversed the base of the dip, toward the truncated eastern end of the fold, discharging into the gouged channels of the breached chalk ridge. The hilltop on the chalk mass at the north eastern end of Thanet overlooked the great Thames-Rhine confluence to the north and east and beyond where groups of human hunter-gatherers ranged over a great dry northern plain which would eventually become the North Sea[8].

As the earth warmed at the beginning of the present Holocene interglacial, the ice sheets retreated to the north, and sea levels rose with steady rapidity (Figure 6.2). Advancing from the west and north, the sea drowned the Channel River, forming the English Channel. No humans recorded their experiences as their familiar coastlines, landmarks and hunting grounds, progressively succumbed to the water, forcing communities to move ever upwards in the landscape as their range was constrained. Eventually, the sea infiltrated the northern river channel, on the west side of Thanet and the eastern mouth of the dip on the southern side of Thanet. Waves washed into the rolling chalk valleys, scouring away the soft debris that had been left in the valleys by meltwash and frost action and eroding the deposits of windblown sand which had blown over the tundra during the last glacial maximum.

6.1

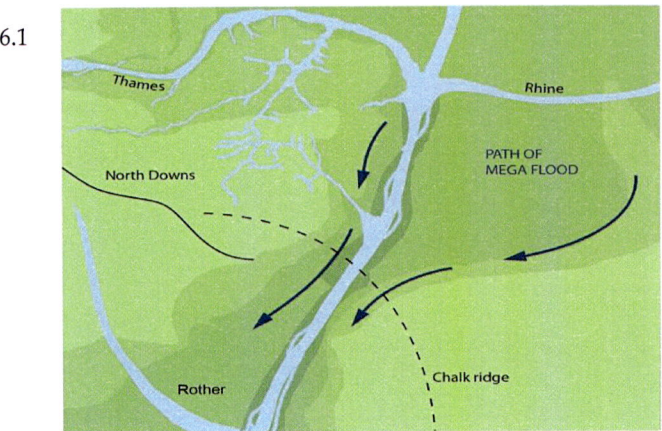

6.2

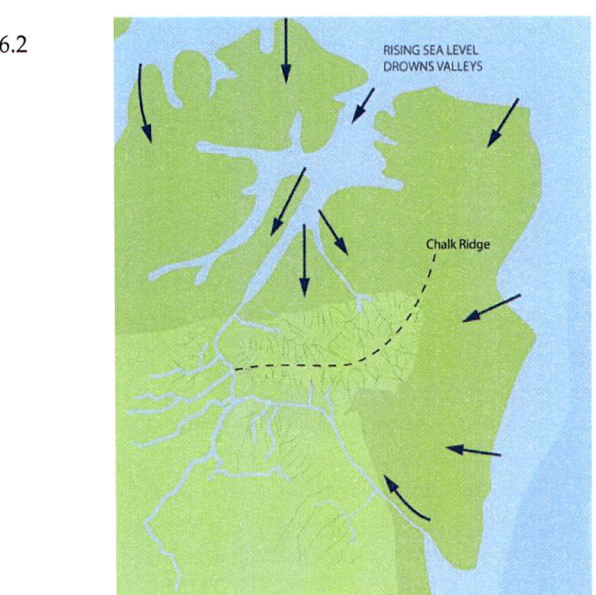

Figure 6. Formation of the Isle of Thanet and Wantsum.

Projecting from reconstructions of the historic sea levels, it may only have been in the Bronze Age, around 2000 BC, that the Wantsum Valley became a significant watercourse, with tides flowing from the Thames estuary and the English Channel into the two linked valleys on the south and west side of Thanet that would form the Wantsum[9].

Around 100 BC, in the late Iron Age, the rate of increase of the sea level slowed and the tides stabilised close to present level[10]. The forces acting on the coastline changed from the rapid submerging of the land by the rising water, to the attrition of the landmass by the sustained force of wave power operating at a constant level. Storm waves drove shingle into the face of the chalk slopes, cutting a shelf around the isolated chalk promontory and forming cliffs at the coast, gradually shaping the island of Thanet. Where the mouth of the Wantsum valley intersected the English Channel, the projecting chalk promontories to the north and south were eroded, creating a widely curved bay between Deal to the south and Cliffsend to the north, with a shallow sloped shelf where the sea entered the valley.

The Stonar beach

McKenny Hughes and George Dowker both suggested that the formation of the beach extending from Cliffsend, southwards to Stonar, relied on the action of a counter current, in opposition to the prevailing west to east flow of the English Channel, to allow the bank to grow from north to south. Recent observations suggest that it was in fact a storm beach or bay bar, a coastal formation recognised as common where shallow water covers a gently sloping platform[11]. When a strong wind is orientated with the axis of the platform, storm waves drive shingle up the slope, creating a bar along the upper limit of the capacity of the wave force to propel the stones up the ramp. In conditions of rising sea levels, earlier beaches that may form at a lower point on the slope are overwashed and destroyed by the increasing power of the waves, leaving no trace behind. The shingle storm beach extended in a long strip from Cliffsend and terminated in a wide bulge at its southern end at Stonar. The final position of the bar, curving between the two chalk rises on the east and west sides of the bay, rests at the historic limit of wave power generated by favourable storm winds rolling up the shelf at the point when sea levels finally stabilised. At high tide in the English

Channel, the rising sea, spring and river flows flooded the inner lagoon formed behind the beach, spreading over the base of the valley. The lagoon was sheltered by the storm beach from the destructive action of waves that operated on the outer coastal area.

The southern spit

At the southern end of the bay, stable sea levels allowed deposits of shingle to build under the action of long shore drift. A spit began to extend northwards from the coast at Deal, growing with a slight curve to the east where deposition at the northern tip of the shingle contended with the flow of pent up tide and river water from the mouth of the lagoon behind the storm beach. Gradually the shingle forced the mouth of the lagoon northward, eventually pushing the opening north of the gap in the earlier beach to form a loop around the southern tip. The older beach was now a fossil relic of an earlier process, gradually being absorbed into the new bank (see Fig.1).

Navigability of the Wantsum

The navigability of the Wanstum depended on several dynamic processes. In the present day, tides rise and fall in the Thames estuary at the north mouth of the Wantsum valley at a slightly different time to those in the English Channel at the eastern mouth, creating a reciprocal difference in tidal potential between the north and east mouths of the Wantsum over the tidal cycle[12]. When the two components of the Wantsum were both open to the sea, this could have produced a scouring swash of tidal water through the channel, the sea flowing from the eastern mouth through the channel to the northern mouth at the flood, then in the reverse direction from the north toward eastern end where the ebb was slightly earlier. The two components of the Wantsum previously described, intersected at Sarre, where an ancient land route terminated on mainland Kent and was taken up again along the ridge across Thanet. John Lewis quoted the antiquary John Twyne, who had suggested that the name Sarre derived from the Latin for a 'saw', as the tides mimicked the reciprocating backward and forward action of a wood saw[13]. At Sarre, located mid-way between Richborough and Reculver, *'the western ebb gave way to the eastern flood, and again the eastern ebb gave place to the western flood'*.

The tides ebbing and flooding through the channel were mediated by the depth and shape of the channel. The outer limits of the floodplain established by examining the maps and elevation survey show that there were a number of narrow constrictions in the valley, where any river or tidal flows would have been constrained. The channel was made up of wide lagoons and narrow pinch points. The broadest sections of the alluvial plain measuring 2.8km from Minster to the opposite side near Wingham and nearly the same width between Down Barton on the east side and west side near Chislet. The narrowest gaps are between Sarre and Wall End, measuring only 1.7km wide and the gap between Chambers Wall and the opposite bank on west side which is only 1.6km wide.

The narrow width of the gap recognised at Sarre already suggests that tidal flow through here would have been complex and this is borne out by Lewis who recorded that the tides met here *'but not fully, nor with equal force, nor at like hours'*[14]. Because of the reciprocating tides the currents, what Lewis called *'the greatest recourse of the stream'* were strongest in the channel here but, because of the variations in the synchronisation of the tides, the swash effect would be neither uniform nor always benevolent.

These irregular and unsynchronised tidal effects operating in the Wantsum suggest that a steady flow of tide or traffic is not a condition we should take for granted and that the interplay of tide and current at Sarre would have played a key role in mediating traffic from land and sea.

Extreme weather

Extreme weather effects have not generally been taken into account in the historical descriptions of the formation and eventual failure of the flow through the Wantsum from the north mouth to the east. One effect of the sea filling the North Sea basin was the occasional, but not permanent, inundation by the sea under the influence of very extreme weather conditions which affected the two entrances to the Wantsum differently.

The predominant influence on the northern entrance to the valley was the dynamics of the greater Thames Estuary. The wide entrance to the

Thames to the east of the mouth of the Wantsum funnelled the North Sea tides, buffering the northern entrance from the direct effects of the sea. The northern mouth was not immune to erosion as the ancient sea bed deposits that were settled in the greater basin of the Thames were washed away with great rapidity, enlarging the estuary. The northern mouth of the Wanstum was vulnerable to storm surges that pushed up the Thames estuary. With the wind blowing from the north, generating maximum fetch in the North Sea, tidal surges are occasionally generated which follow a predicable circuit, running down the east coast of Britain before wheeling around to the east, along the coast of Northern France and the Netherlands[15]. Surges funnelled up the Thames estuary, periodically threatened to flood the banks of the river far along its course and any tributaries, inundating many normally relatively dry areas and flooding the marshes along the side of the river.

The effect of a storm surge into the north mouth of the Wantsum Channel was most recently demonstrated by the devastating floods that occurred after a wave front almost 1.5 metres above normal high tide was forced up the Thames estuary in 1953[16]. Breaching the sea defences that had been established across the former northern entrance to the Wantsum valley between Birchington and Reculver, the swollen estuary surged over the flat levels that had formed when the channels of the north mouth had silted, the ground had been reclaimed with embankments and the marshes had been drained in the 18th century. In 1953 the flood water reached as far as Brooksend Farm, but, local newspapers report[17], did not cross the Canterbury road, which was raised on a slight platform stopping the water penetrating further into the deep valley to the east of the farm.

The limits of the flood did not exceed the limits of the alluvial plain established at the contour 1.5m above Ordnance Datum and the evidence of the 1953 flood suggests that historically this had always been the limit of storm surges recorded or unrecorded in the past.

Silt deposited by storm surges may have been one of the major causes of the eventual failure of the tidal flows from the north mouth which was substantially blocked, except for a series of interlaced channels and silted loops by the time the earliest map of the area was published in 1548[18]. The traditional date for the failure of the flow through the

Wantsum is recorded as 1462, in a popular tradition recorded by John Lewis, coinciding with the construction Tenterden steeple. Flooding is recorded in the Thames in 1570, reaching as far as Erith and coinciding with the devastating All Saints flood in the Netherlands. The silt from this flood and its predecessors possibly contributed to the final failure of the reciprocal flow through the channel[19]. The alluvial limits of the Wantsum that can be traced on the Ordnance Map probably reflect the limits of this periodic flooding rather than the usual extents of the navigable waters of the Wantsum.

The eastern mouth of the Wantsum was more vulnerable to storm waves of unusual strength coming from the English Channel. Periodically waves would have submerged and breached the inner shingle spit at high tide, exposing the inner lagoon to wave damage and causing widespread flooding of the flats and marshes on the plain on the southern side of Thanet. In 1365 a north easterly storm nearly destroyed the town of Stonar, which had grown up on the wide southern tip of the inner shingle bank[20]. Destruction by the encroaching waves on the eastern side of Thanet brought down the chalk cliffs in periodic falls and left valleys that once had access to the sea hanging in the cliff line. When Lewis suggested that Cotmanfield had been within the reach of the sea at the time of Augustine's landing, it is possible that the storm beach had been more substantial in that area in the 6th century and had been suited as a harbour, as many sites on the eastern coast line had been in the Roman period. The storm attrition gradually necessitated the construction of the Boarded Groin to preserve the east facing edge of the Ebbsfleet peninsula.

The location of landing places

The dynamics of the Thames estuary prevailed over the northern section of the Wantsum; the English Channel system prevailed on the eastern section. With the tidal rises and falls at either end, the effect of the waves rolling up a shallow chalk platform at its eastern mouth, and the periodic catastrophic extension of the Thames estuary into one of its rarer channels, contributed to making the Wantsum an unpredictable location, with margins that were not firmly defined. Transit through the Wantsum could only be made by careful management of the circumstances of tide and time. Large accumulations of mud and silt would have formed at the tidal margins forming flats and salt marshes that were relatively dry for much of the time. Periodically, depending on the weather conditions, a storm surge would rush in to the north mouth, flooding wider lagoon north of Sarre. At the eastern mouth unusually strong storm waves could scour the ancient beach away and flood the lagoon.

Boats could not, as has been suggested, freely navigate through the Wantsum channel to reach the Thames, they would have to lay up waiting for the correct moment, or break their cargos and reload on to smaller, more suitable ships, or perhaps unload their cargos on the landing stages for land transport. The interplay of tides in the water course suggests that the havens afforded by smaller fleets, where the outflow of springs on the flanking valleys intersected with the main flow of the Stour and Wantsum rivers, would have variable utility, which could be exploited by different types of craft with different cargo capacities.

It has been suggested that the loss of daylight following the long crossing of the Dover Strait would have made a stop overnight at the entrance to the Wantsum necessary before it could be navigated[21]. Another analysis has pointed out that, for sailed vessels, winds that were favourable to north easterly navigation along the coast to reach the eastern mouth, would not have been favourable to the westerly route through the entrance to the channel, and again a layover at the entrance to wait for the wind to change may have been necessary[22]. In these circumstances, and following a long voyage, Augustine may have preferred an immediate disembarkation rather than stay in the ship waiting to sail further on.

These natural nodes within the Wantsum Valley river navigation system give us clues about why communities were located at key points in Thanet throughout history. These places would have had advantages over the cycle of the tides through the channel and been significant to commerce, or the control of traffic and goods by river transport, the communities established at the fleet mouths and particularly at the important tidal junction at Sarre and the strategic point at Richborough overlooking the entrance to the inner lagoon, having a great importance within the navigable channel as a whole. By understanding where the nodes in the network are, represented by the location of the Fleets and the possible siting of havens and ports, we can begin to frame a geographic context for Augustine's first contact with the people of Kent.

REVIEWING THE CULTURAL CONTEXT

Pope Gregory and Rome

Central to the story of Augustine's mission to Britain is Pope Gregory I who prevailed on Augustine to travel from Rome to what had been the most distant province of the old Empire[1]. Descended from an ancient and noble Roman family, Gregory had served as prefect of the city of Rome and as an ambassador for the Holy See of Rome, to the Imperial Court at Byzantium (now Istanbul) where in the early 4th century AD, the Emperor Constantine had founded a new Rome in the East, renamed Constantinople[2]. The political and cultural centre of the Roman Empire moved to Byzantium, which was Greek in language and culture, altering the whole character and culture of the Empire which was reinforced by Constantine's adoption of Christianity as the official state religion. Although with diminishing territories, Constantinople and the Byzantine Empire survived as a direct link to the culture of Imperial Rome until the siege and capture of the city by the Ottoman Sultan Mehmet II in 1453.

Recent considerations of the history of Europe in the period after the nominal dissolution of the Western Roman Empire in 476 AD, emphasise the continuity of a form of Roman culture within the Byzantine city and state, the real or imagined power of the Eastern Roman Emperor and his court exerted an influence on the states that succeeded Roman Imperial power in the West. Although the new Germanic kingdoms brought their own cultural ideas to the structure of power, their leaders were flattered to receive official titles from the Imperial Court, favouring them over the traditional ranks of their own cultures. The influence extended into the material culture of the new kingdoms, objects once thought as defining an alien 'barbarian' culture, can now be seen as having continuity with the Roman past through their own Roman heritage and through their links to the Byzantine Empire.

In later years, suffering from a chronic illness and wanting to take on the contemplative discipline of life as a monk, Gregory converted an urban Villa, owned by his family and located on the Caelian Hill, the south easternmost of the seven hills enclosed within the walls of Rome, into a monastery dedicated to St. Andrew under the Benedictine rule. He entered the tough life of work and prayer as the Abbott between 575 and 580. Gregory was compelled to return to worldly concerns when he became the Bishop of Rome, and head of the Roman Catholic Church in 590, serving until his death in 602.

Before the western half of the Roman Empire was dissolved, the seat of power in the west had moved to Ravenna on the east coast of Italy, closer to Constantinople, the centre of power in the East. Although in Gregory's time much of Italy was ruled by enclaves of Germanic Lombards, large regions, including Rome, remained under the administration of a governor appointed by the Byzantine Emperor, the Exarch of Ravenna. Although nominally under the authority of the Exarch, the Bishops of Rome had taken over much of the administrative control of the region around Rome. By taking control of the supply of the physical and spiritual needs of the people within his territories, and by extension into the Barbarian Kingdoms, Gregory began to assert the independence of Rome from the Exarch and the Eastern Empire. With a diminishing population, Rome was becoming a fortified medieval citadel, rather than the hub of Empire it had formerly been[3].

Bede reports that shortly before his appointment as Bishop, Gregory himself had wished to make the journey to Britain to convert of the Angles, after encountering slave boys from the northern British Kingdom of Deira which by the 6th century extended from the Humber to the Tees, on sale in the Roman Forum[4]. Instead he appointed Augustine, a monk in his own Monastery to lead the mission to Britain. Gregory's experience at the Imperial court undoubtedly influenced the diplomatic skills he employed in his Papacy and in his attempts to extend the power of the Roman church in western Europe. As Augustine travelled, he brought introductory letters from Gregory and gifts for each of the Bishops of the cities he stayed with, and for the rulers of the Frankish Kingdoms he passed through along the way. Gregory's letters urged them to support and protect Augustine's mission with practical assistance. The formality of the introductory letters and the gifts Augustine carried to give to each recipient, reflected the rituals of diplomacy that were current in the Byzantine court and were, in origin, rooted in the habits of Classical Rome.

In the 6th century the city of Rome remained a symbol of enduring authority, influencing the political outlook of the new kingdoms growing out of the provinces and regions of the Empire as ancient titles and honours remained attractive.

The Romanisation of Britain

Augustine came from a different Roman tradition to that bequeathed to the former British province, he was sent from a monastery in the heart of the ancient city which, although much diminished, still retained a degree of prosperity and sophistication and enjoyed connections with the surviving Eastern section of the Empire which still remained economically and militarily strong.

Roman Britain had been a very different place to the great continental provinces of the Roman Empire, particularly the cosmopolitan cities and the vast landed estates. In many respects much of what was distinctively Roman about the province of Britannia had been imported and sustained by the presence of a disproportionately large regular army. The garrison towns, forts and outposts of the army were the centres of Romano-British life style and were sustained by the cash imported to pay regular wages and special donations to the troops. This Roman influenced culture never quite threw off all its pre-Roman roots and influences. Britain was inhibited in its capacity to develop a Mediterranean classical culture by its location beyond the continental land mass on the periphery of Empire. Contact with Britain required a maritime capability, which, if control from the continent was to be enforced, had to be strong, reliable and loyal, three conditions that were not consistently met by the Roman Navy, or the Army.

The major Roman continental ports of East Kent were located at Lympne, Dover and in the vicinity of Richborough, from these, a network of roads linked the ports to Canterbury, the principal Roman town[5]. Located at the base of a deep valley cutting through great white cliffs Dover was perhaps suited as a deep water port for sea going ships. Lympne and Richborough were both located in low lying areas, creeks and flats were screened by shingle banks. There may have been several possible landing places within the immediate area of the creeks. Many minor sea ports may have existed in Kent, which have either been lost to coastal erosion or hidden beneath drifting shingle and mud that has been deposited since the Roman period. Archaeological evidence suggests that other sea ports in Thanet are likely to have been located at the valley bases along the cliffs of the east coast of Thanet, at Ramsgate, at Stone Bay north of Broadstairs and as far north east as Kingsgate[6]. These havens have since been destroyed by relentless erosion of the cliffs by the sea. On the north coast of Thanet, in the Thames estuary there were ports on the Thames estuary at Margate, possibly at Birchington and Westgate, and at Reculver on the west coast of the Wantsum[7].

In the late 3rd century AD, the commander of the Roman naval fleet in Britain began construction on a system of maritime forts, which were strategically located to control the sea traffic and the roads to the major towns, had formed the power base of the Roman Army in Britain along the coastline of Kent, Essex and Norfolk, a further defensive line of coastal signal stations extended up the Yorkshire coast[8]. The forts on the Kent coast were located at the major continental ports at Lympne, Dover, Richborough and Reculver. Later, under the command of an officer called the Count of the Saxon Shore, these maritime defences, protected the province from sea raiders from the coasts of Germany and Scandinavia, but they also formed a line of defence from continental Romans during a particularly rebellious period which began in the late 3rd century and continued until the province was finally abandoned when Roman armies based in Britain supported several attempts by military commanders to usurp the Imperial Throne[9].

Richborough

Richborough is mentioned by a number of Roman historians and geographers and appears to have been considered the principal port of entry into Roman Britain[10]. The forts and town at Richborough, built in several phases from the invasion in 43 AD until the late 3rd century, occupy a platform of compacted sand raised above the surrounding area overlooking a lagoon, intersected by series of channels fringed by mudflats and marshes. The island that Richborough occupies was strategically significant, overlooking the eastern entrance to the inner lagoon at the eastern end of the Wantsum. At the top of the eastern edge of the island, a town and later the great stone walls of one of the forts under the command of the Count of the Saxon Shore overlooked the haven. In the late 1st century AD a large marble clad monumental arch, standing on four pillars mounted on a deep concrete platform, was erected in the civil settlement, probably to stand as a symbolic gateway to the Island of Britain[11]. From Richborough the Stour gave rapid access by boat to the city of Canterbury, which could also be reached by a road leading from the north west of Richborough and from Wall End opposite Sarre. It was also possible to navigate with favourable tides, around the southern and western sides of the Isle of Thanet, through the Wantsum channel, to the Thames on the northern end but other landing places were located in the channel within the reach of such places as the Villa, or possibly a 'Mansio' guest house, which was located at Minster[12].

Britain after the Romans

Little is recorded of the changes that characterised later Roman Britain and the period following the withdrawal of regular troops from the Island which seems to have taken place in the early 5th century. Archaeology tells us more about the material culture of the period but it is difficult to turn archaeological interpretations into traditional historical narratives.

Rome had changed over the long period of the Empire, the Roman army dispersed many young men from alien cultures around the Empire, partly to prevent them from gaining strength in their own regions and partly to refresh the declining power of soldiers recruited from the Italian mainland, who may have been a relatively small proportion of the forces that were deployed in the name of Rome. The traditional Legionary infantryman largely disappeared from the ranks of the Imperial army after a crisis in the Empire in the third century, the later Roman soldier would have been harder to distinguish in costume and culture from the people of Germany and Scandinavia that historical texts tell us entered Britain as allies[13].

The end of the Roman Empire has been characterised as the victory of the land owning classes over the people of the cities and towns who made their livings through trade and commerce and exercised the power to raise tax and administer the law[14]. The landowner, who controlled the real products of the land and had the right to dispose and distribute the produce among his family and retainers, rose to dominance. Powerful Romans retreated to their estates, under pressure from the taxes imposed on city life by a state that was increasingly pressed to provide soldiers for the protection of borders and to fight internal power struggles. They hired or settled wandering peoples to defend their estates and to provide them with local security and gradually the power of the Roman state to raise troops for payments in cash, which had declined for many years in favour of settlement on land in exchange for service, was dissolved.

In the maritime regions of Britain the power of the landed was enhanced by the trade and military strength that could be supplied from the sea. It is likely that Richborough remained the traditional port of entry to the Island of Britain for both the sea going people of the continent who navigated the channel in the course of their fishing and trading industries and for the dwindling number of official visitors representing the remnants of Imperial power in Western Europe, or the emissaries of the new Kingdoms that succeeded the Roman Empire and claimed to be overlords of the Kings of Kent. In the period of almost two centuries that elapsed between the final abandonment of the Roman province of Britain and Augustine's mission, the progressive migration of the north mouth of the lagoon northwards would have reduced the utility and accessibility of the old Roman port although it was still accessible to reduced traffic from the continent[15].

The estuaries on the north and east of the Wantsum channel, suited the shallow draft of the vessels sailed by the people of Northern Germany and Scandinavia who, even in the Roman period, had started to probe the coastline of Kent and to enter the service of the Roman Army[16]. Once the Roman navies had stopped patrolling the Channel and the entrance to the North Sea, the occasional visits and raids turned into the settlement and conquest that features in the early histories of the Anglo-Saxon people. Eventually the leaders of these people forged Kingdoms and alliances that allowed them to exercise their personal power over large areas of the former Roman province.

What we know of the early years following the loss of Britain to the Roman Empire is confused and, most historians agree, distorted by the mixing of a few garbled historical facts with myths and legends that were drawn from many sources[17]. It was on the maritime fringes of Kent along the banks of the Wantsum channel, and the Isle of Thanet, that were reputed to be the stronghold of the earliest Germanic mercenaries, men brought in to support what one contemporary observer, a British Monk called Gildas who lived through the 6th century (500 – 570) called *'Proud Tyrants'* who tried to usurp what remained of Roman power in Britain[18]. The mercenaries seem to have turned against their masters and built their kingdoms with a mix of old and new arrangements of the disposal of land and people, settlers and British Natives, mixing the old Romano-British culture with the traditions of their own Germanic and Scandinavian heritage.

Anglo-Saxon Kent in 597AD

An important theme in the histories written about the Early Anglo-Saxon Kingdoms of Britain is to what extent the social and economic life of the Roman occupation survived the passing of the Imperial provinces into the hands of local Kings and warlords. In an earlier historical tradition, where classical culture was seen as a force for improving mankind, the end of the Roman Empire was regarded as the start of a 'dark age' of ignorance and chaos where baser instincts prevailed. Historians now question these assumptions, recognising that the skills of metal working and other craft trades that identify the Early-Post Roman culture in Britain were sophisticated and technologically advanced as anything produced in the Roman Empire. The hybrid of the traditions of the Roman culture and that of the peoples who remained outside the Empire, produced a new culture which had new aspects but retained much knowledge of, and the structural form of what had preceded it[19]. As we begin to understand the complexity of post-Roman societies, we begin to understand how they may have been distributed over the landscape, and that far from a free for all grab of the riches of Roman society, many of the customs and traditions of land ownership and social organisation may well have been adapted into the new cultures.

The visible manifestations of this culture have been deduced from the messages that were conveyed by the clothes and items that were left in graves (Plate 1), meant to serve their owners beyond life in the world[20]. We do not know about the lives of those whose graves had little or no goods. They may have had status and privilege that came from another source; culture, wisdom or labour. Burials with arms are certainly well attested from the whole maritime region of east Kent and must have had significance within society[21]. Anglo-Saxon culture is seen as one where bearing arms was a sign of rank, in life and in death; and rank formed the basis of precedent and privilege.

Plate 1. Male with shield excavated at the Ozengell Anglo-Saxon cemetery near Ramsgate in 1982 (Grave 204).

There were no councils of Townsmen, making their living through trade and joining together to pass laws to be applied to the country, to meet Augustine. There were only powerful men whose authority lay in retaining a personal retinue of soldiers, servants and advisors, who were sustained by consuming the food and supplies that the labourers and peasants in their estates were obliged by custom to hand over for storage and distribution. Powerful men dominated lesser men, but themselves owed service to greater men. Society was linked by customary obligations for service, protection and exchange of goods.

The obligations of service prevailed within the Kingdoms and extended between the Kingdoms of the eastern sea board of Britain. Aethelbert's overlordship was said by Bede to extend as far as the Humber[22]. The territory he controlled was not dissimilar to that of the Roman Count of the Saxon Shore, who controlled the forts on the same coast that formed the power base of the Roman navy and land army in the later Empire.

Part of Aethelbert's power lay in the dramatic expression of Kingship, founded on personal charisma and dynastic authority, some of which derived from an origin myth which combined the claim of descent from Hengist and Horsa, the Horse and Mare that may represent a mythological symbol of fertility; the association of his dynastic name 'Oiscing' with the Ash tree was also a symbol of natural power[23]. The myths emphasised the might of hand that had released the Saxons from the service of the Britons and made them masters of their own territories in the Island.

The continuous physical assertion of the King's right over land and goods was made by constant progression of the Royal entourage through the kingdom, consuming the dues from the produce of the land in the feasting halls of his palaces, the 'Villa Regalis', located in each of the sub-regions of the Royal territory. Aethelbert's palaces were great timber framed halls, located among the large villages that formed the centres of population within his kingdom. Each year the Royal household would progress around the county from hall to hall, consuming the grain, mead, honey, firewood, metal, leather, wax and a myriad of other consumables that were due from the subordinates that he allowed to occupy and administer his estates. In turn these goods were extracted by the estate managers from the villagers and agricultural peasants who tilled the land and produced the goods that were due.

We can gain some understanding of the scale of the buildings at these estate centres from the remains of a timber framed hall, measuring 21 by 8.5 metres, recently discovered by archaeologists at Lyminge near Canterbury[24]. The Lyminge hall was probably within a Royal estate complex, possibly contemporary with Aethelbert's reign, which later became a monastery. The hall is close to the site of a Roman Villa which it may have succeeded as a centre where the produce of the surrounding estates were consumed.

The relationships of power and precedence structuring the early Anglo-Saxon Kingdoms were expressed by personal proximity to the King in the hierarchy of his retinue, in his assemblies, councils and in the mead halls. Decisions would be made in meetings of the most important retainers, officials and representatives of other interests. At these meetings charters would be witnessed and ratified and laws given by the King and approved by the assemblies.

The maritime regions of Britain remained in contact with the ancient Rhine Trade Route which had served the regions from prehistoric times. These contacts are reflected in the importation of Lava Querns and an abundance of glass vessels, manufactured in the workshops of the Rhine which had operated since Roman times. Kent's early Saxon kingdom's were linked through the continental kingdoms of the Franks to the remnant of the surviving elements of the culture of the Roman world and to the wider post imperial cultures of Europe which mixed Roman and Germanic cultural elements with the still prospering Eastern Empire of Byzantium, which was continuous with the Imperial Roman state[25]. Aethelbert's wife Bertha was the daughter Charibert I, the Merovingian King of Paris.

Kentish Graves of the 6th and 7th century were richly furnished with clothing, weapons, jewellery, pottery and glassware, coins and personal items, many of the graves discovered in the Anglo-Saxon cemeteries on Thanet and along the western side of the Wantsum contain items which were manufactured on the continent. Later graves contain wheel thrown pottery vessels manufactured in the Frankish Kingdom and imported in some quantity to Kent[26].

With its eclectic mix of costume, derived in part from the Anglo-Saxon homelands but also from other traditions including those of the Merovingian and Byzantine Courts, Kent's emerging culture has been likened to a pirate community, borrowing, looting and adapting from those around it[27]. Aethelbert's power, as pirate King of these maritime people, extended over the havens of the eastern coast of England from Yorkshire to Kent, not through his ability to hold large tracts inland but through the control of the river mouths and trading ports of coastal regions. Aethelbert was not the tribal King of a Jutish people, he was

ANGLO SAXON ANTIQUITIES FROM SARR.

Figure 7. Items accompanying a woman buried in the Anglo-Saxon cemetery at Sarre, excavated in 1862 (Grave 4).

King of Kent, the region that grown out of the combined cultures of Imperial Rome, German and Scandinavian traditions of the exercise of power and the machinations of the Franks, the continental neighbours who still exerted claims over the distant province[28]. His power lay in the exercise of authority through alliance, kinship and, where necessary, force. His authority had to be continuously asserted or it would be lost to any one of the competing minor kingdoms that surrounded his territory, or to a retainer who saw a chance to take power for himself. Some understanding of the dramatic personality of a contemporary pagan King can be gained from the example of the grave goods in contemporary Royal burials. The richly furnished burial chamber within the hull of a ship, buried under a great mound, at Sutton Hoo in East Anglia, is possibly the tomb of King Raedwald, a contemporary andsubordinate of Aethelbert's. Among the items at Sutton Hoo were silver bowls, richly decorated drinking vessels and objects such a large mounted whetstone which has been interpreted as a ceremonial sceptre[29]. Along with the powerful indigenous symbols of the King's own maritime culture, warrior prowess and physical dominance, these objects demonstrate the sophisticated links between the English Kings and the continental Kingdoms and also with Rome and Byzantium. A similar richly furnished tomb chamber, possibly the grave of Saebert a King of Essex who died in 616 AD, was found in 2003 at Prittlewell near Southend[30]. If, as Bede implies, Raedwald and Saebert were Aethelbert's subordinates, how much more impressive might he have appeared in their company?

When Augustine and his company, numbering as many as 40, entered the marshy coastline of Kent, they sailed into a harbour from which the last organised Roman troops in Britain had been withdrawn nearly two centuries ago. Among the flocks and villages of the downland, and the streams and marches that reached back from the beaches on the coast, the walls of the great Saxon Shore fortresses at Richborough and Reculver still rose from islands raised among the marshes, relics of a last struggle for the defence of the maritime borders of the northern part of the Roman Empire. They were entering a territory which had a well organised system of agricultural production distribution that supported a hierarchical society. Power in this territory came from rights to a share of the product of the land, a network of estates and collecting centres controlled the production and distribution of food, saltings processed and preserved the produce of the sea. Along the ridge stretched an ancient trackway, crossing the Wantsum at a ford or causeway near Sarre, and on the western side followed the southern edge of the Stour Valley to Canterbury, linking the easternmost limit of southern Britain to the main hinterland of the province[31].

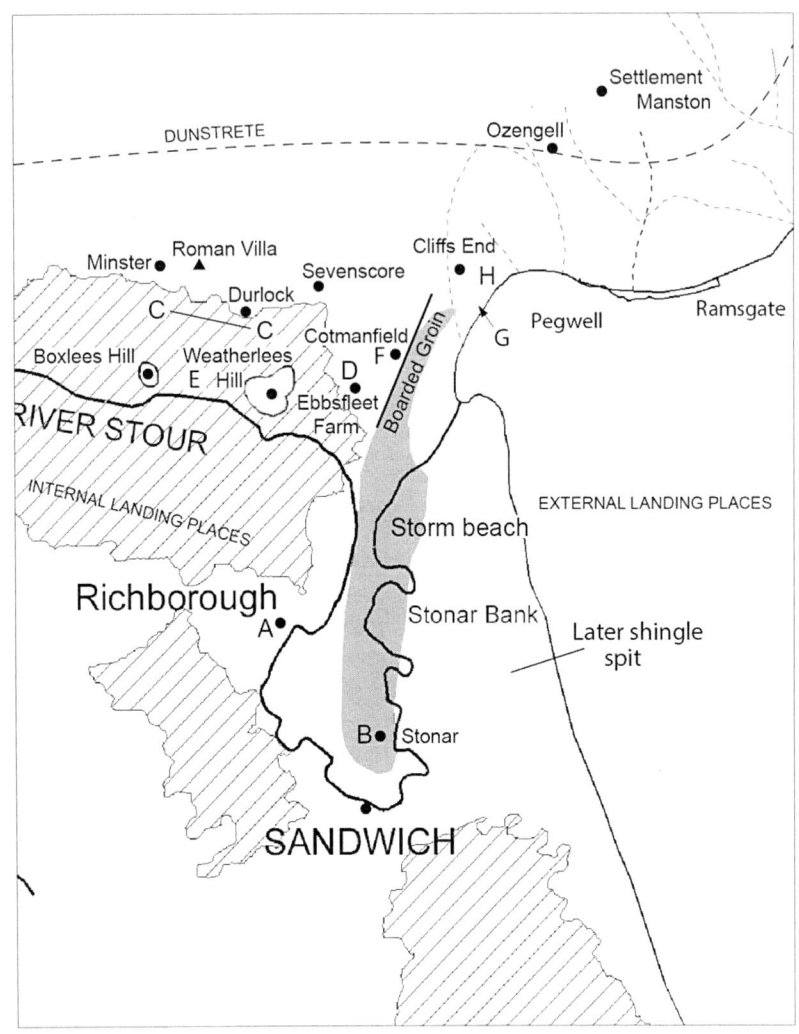

Figure 8. Location of possible landing places.

THE LANDING

To reconsider the possible sites of the first landing place of Augustine it will be helpful to return to our best source, Bede, and examine his narrative against new evidence on the geographical and cultural context of Augustine's landing.

The following schematic sequence of events for the landing on Thanet is given authority by a close reading of Bede's narrative[1] (Appendix 1):

1. Augustine came ashore (Location 1 – shore), with his companions, numbering about forty men, including the Frankish translators they had taken on.

2. Augustine sent word to Aethelbert [who was therefore not in the immediate area] informing him that he had come from Rome.

3. When Aethelbert heard the message, he ordered Augustine's group to remain in the Island and ordered that supplies were given to the group until he decided what to do with them (they must have been in a place where substantial supplies were available, or have been moved to another location where they could be found - possible Location 2 – somewhere near a supply store).

4. After some days [while Augustine waited for him at location 1 or 2] Aethelbert came to the Isle of Thanet (by land or possibly by sea).

5. Aethelbert took his seat in the open air (Location 3) and ordered Augustine to come there and confer with him and his courtiers (an assembly, formal or informal).

6. Augustine's group came to the meeting place bearing a silver cross as their standard and a picture of Christ (formally presenting themselves as monks and followers of Christ).

7. At the King's bidding Augustine's group preached to the assembly (making their case to the assembly).

8. Bede reports that in reply Aethelbert acknowledged that they came in good faith and sincerely believed the words they spoke, having come a long way to do so, but because what was said was new and unproven he could not abandon what [the ideas or religion] he held in common with the English people [*Anglorum Gente*] (i.e. he was unable to commit his people to an unproven faith on his own account).

9. Wanting to be kind to Augustine's party, Aethelbert agreed that he would give them any necessary supplies and would not prevent them preaching or converting any people they could (raising no objection to his people converting individually).

10. Aethelbert gave Augustine's group lodgings in Canterbury [Doruuerensi], given by Bede as the capital [Metropolis] of his empire [imperii] (but this was perhaps as someone with experience of the Roman church, which was organised on the continent by cities, saw the location in the old city). Bede later explains that the monks established themselves as a monastic community in the lodgings they were given in Canterbury.

Bede's text gives us the authority for at least two, possibly three separate locations for the activities of Augustine's group in the first days of the mission; the initial disembarkation site, where they may have waited for some days before they met with the King; possibly a second site where the large party might have been taken so they could be supplied for the wait and finally a meeting place where they were able to meet Aethelbert and present their mission to him and his court.

Previous authors have considered the problem of the location of St. Augustine's first landing as if it took place in a deserted landscape, the choice of site being among locations whose physical circumstances afforded a reasonable landing, but without considering the social context. We must at least take into account that there may have been ships of Aethelbert's own fleet and those of the surrounding community in the port, not to say those of continental traders and other distant visitors. In a maritime culture it must have been common for people to arrive in a port unannounced, whose intentions would need to be investigated. A ship might arrive with a cargo whose port dues needed to be established or are disputed. The crew of a contemporary oared, plank built long-ship, like that found at Mound 1 at Sutton Hoo, or the one found in another burial mound at Snape in East Anglia, whether used for cargo or as a warship, would number as many as 30 men, and Augustine's ship's company was certainly of that order[2]. The Anglo-Saxon kings were only too aware of what a hostile crew sailing into those waters was capable of. A form of naval diplomacy and formal hospitality must have been in place in Aethelbert's ports to meet such circumstances.

It has been suggested that the very rich 6th and 7th century graves that have been excavated at a large cemetery at Sarre and at Buckland in Dover, where there were unusually high numbers of weapon burials, represented the military establishment of a Port Reeve, a Royal officer in charge of maritime military and civil issues[3]. Such an officer may have controlled the confluence of road, river and sea routes at the constriction in the Wantsum channel at Sarre, which imposed physical limits on the passing of maritime traffic and where the major land routes could be intercepted. If a port Reeve with troops was present at Sarre, the ports must have had a customary practice for receiving unexpected guests. There may have been some sort of customs holding area where the intentions of visitors and the contents of ships could be identified for the purpose of preventing the entry of undesirable people or securing the correct taxation. We may not need to look for a camp site on a river bank for Augustine but a customs quarantine area for the port. We can assume that the arrival, disembarkation and progress of Augustine's entourage through the hierarchy of Aethelbert's court would have been carefully managed, and took place in a carefully chosen location that would deprive the Roman Monks of any potential to exert any physical or mysterious powers. Taking into account the period between announcing their arrival to Aethelbert and waiting for him to come to Thanet, which is related in Bede's account, we should not look for a central place for the first landing of Augustine and his company but one that was more functional to the maritime gateways to Aethelbert's kingdom. It is likely therefore that Augustine's first landing place was somewhere neutral, which would not prejudice the deliberation of the meeting that was to take place, or which would not allow him, as with any other unknown visitor arriving with a large company of men aboard ship, to establish any advantage for themselves physical or supernatural.

Knowing the key locations within the network of accessible locations in the Wantsum we can begin to set out the more detailed parameters for the physical location of the disembarkation, where it would have been proper for St Augustine to land as he entered Aethelbert's Kingdom. Some locations were identified by previous authors, within the interior of the lagoon and on the east side of Thanet that could be reached by boat from the sea:

The first is the island at Richborough with its defensive walls, which was favoured by many of the Canterbury chroniclers (Fig. 8, **A**). Against this is Bede's clear assertion that the landing place was in Thanet, Richborough was until very recently, clearly separated by the lagoon and large areas of mudflats or marshes from Thanet and because of its defensive role in the Wantsum estuary it may not have been a port suited to general traffic.

Stonar, the important twin port on the opposite side of the river mouth to Richborough, later claimed by the port of London, was favoured by George Dowker as the location for Augustine's landing (Fig. 8, **B**). Was there an appropriate facility on Stonar to receive Augustine? There certainly may have been a military facility at the site in the Roman period, which might have had a successor in a timber hall for receiving newly arrived visitors to the port. As Dowker argued, Stonar is conceivably sufficiently connected to Thanet to satisfy Bede's narrative, linked by the shingle beach to the mainland at Cliffsend.

Dowker thought there could have been a landing somewhere within the Minster Fleet, where the streams from the hillside springs at Minster and Durlock/Sevenscore, flowed out between raised islands at Weatherlees and Boxlees and met the tidal waters of the lagoon (Fig. 8, **C**). It could be argued that, by coincidence, the location now called Ebbsfleet where there would have been a sloping beach or flats on the western side of the Ebbsfleet peninsula, is a good candidate for a first landing place for Augustine and his party (Fig. 8, **D**). This place, where there had once been an important Iron Age and Roman settlement, linked the lagoon to the hinterland of Thanet and undoubtedly could been used by the local community to pull up the small boats used to navigate around the lagoon and the Stour and Wantsum valleys. Augustine could have been rowed from his large vessel, moored in the central channel of the lagoon, to a beaching on the western side of the peninsula, to wait for the King to respond to his message, or into the spring fed basin at Durlock or Sevenscore, in the lower reaches of the valley that flanks the western side of the peninsula.

It is possible that Augustine could have been rowed from his ship to one of the two large islands in the eastern lagoon of the estuary, deserted because of their association with the ancient dead, and surrounded by the broad mudflats and streams of the lagoon (Fig. 8.). Encamped on one of these islands for a few days, within a space which belonged neither to the land or the sea, Augustine may have waited for the King's response to his messengers.

John Lewis considered the landing place, which he called Ebbsfleet, to be located on the east side of the shingle beach leading from Stonar, somewhere between the rise of the peninsula and the beginning of the cliff line at Cliffsend (Fig. 8, **F**), where he suggested the sea met the shore along what is now Cottington Lane. The northern end of the great storm beach seems to have been vulnerable to damage by the coastal erosion suffered by the whole Pegwell Bay region. Steps had been taken by the Abbott of St. Augustine's Abbey in 1280 to prevent stone being removed from the shingle beach, which was re-enforced at some time by a sea wall known as the Boarded Groin[4]. This location had been rejected in the past, on the principal that beaching through the surf on this shore would have been undignified for the Roman party. However it is likely that the erosion checked by the Boarded Groin, had not progressed so far at the time and they may have come to shore on a more substantial sloping storm beach, with little or no trouble relative to the discomfort of the journey as a whole. It is this site which is currently marked by the Ordnance Survey as the location of Augustine's landing, and that of the earlier Saxon ships of Hengist.

The geography of the eastern coast of the Isle of Thanet and the Wantsum channel dictates two broad choices in deciding between the possible locations of landing sites for Augustine. The first is that his ship sailed through what has been established as the narrow outlet of the inner lagoon, sheltered by the Stonar shingle beach, to allow the travellers to disembark at one of the landing places within the lagoon or on the smaller fleets that led from the central channel (Fig. 8, Inner Landing Places). The second is that sea ports remained open on the eastern seaward side of the Isle of Thanet, as they had in Roman times, giving access to a series of deep valleys that lead up to the ancient track that crossed Thanet's chalk plateau[5] (Fig. 8, External Landing Places).

The limited evidence we have from historical texts; along with the analysis of the complexity of the navigation through the Wantsum, particularly the suggestion that the mouth of the channel could not be entered immediately after a channel crossing; as well as the discoveries of contemporary archaeological sites, suggest that the balance of probability is with a landing at a port on the outer coast, on the eastern side of Thanet.

The last survivors of the outer ports are the bays at Broadstairs and the more significant port at Ramsgate which remains open to sizeable ships.

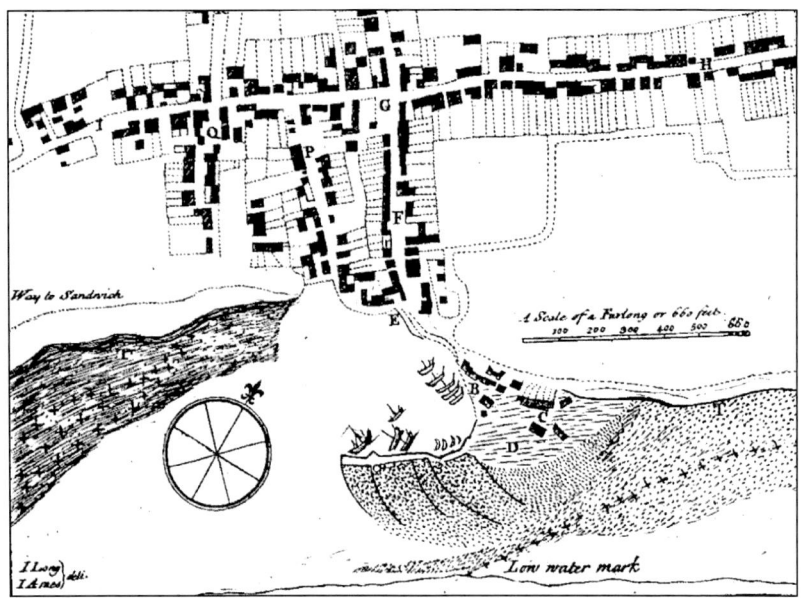

Figure 8. Extract of Abbot and Spencer's map of Ramsgate c. 1723 showing gravel bank forming eastern side of harbour.

Ramsgate itself was founded in the shelter of a sweeping shingle bank which protected a south facing bay until the stone piers of the harbour were built in the mid 19th century[6] (Fig. 9). Storm shingle banks continue to accumulate on the wave cut platform north of the harbour (Plate 2). Further south in the later 6th century, in the area where the Boarded Groin would be built, another port may have been equally accessible at the confluence of dry valleys at Pegwell Bay, the mouth of the bay sealed with the sloping shingle bank of the storm beach, not yet cut away by erosion and rare prodigious scouring storms (Fig. 8, **G**).

The party could have been intercepted and temporarily accommodated at a guest hall, possibly near Cliffsend (Fig. 8, **H**) where contemporary archaeological features have been found suggesting that reasonable sized village may have existed here, where shellfish were processed in great abundance[7]. At the southern end of the cliff line of Pegwell Bay, a small 6th century Anglo-Saxon cemetery of 21 graves stood on an

Plate 2. Storm shingle bank exposed at low tide off Ramsgate, winter 2012. © G. A. Moody.

isolated hill, where once Bronze Age burial mounds had been raised to overlook the valley below[8]. Further up the broad hollow cutting through the downland there is the large, 6th and 7th century cemetery at Ozengell, Ramsgate; built over a complex of prehistoric burial monuments and located on the ancient ridge road of Dunstrete, which leads across Thanet's chalk plateau[9]. Further to the north of the cemetery at Ozengell is one of the few attested contemporary settlements discovered by archaeologists[10]. On the upper reaches of the western side of the hollow, adjacent to the ridge road is the first of a series of rich Anglo-Saxon cemeteries that, like their Roman antecedents, line the ridge in regularly spaced groups from east to the west, ending at the great cemetery at Sarre, where the ridge road intersects with the Wantsum[11]. From this site, Augustine could have taken the road along the chalk ridge to meet Aethelbert at his chosen location.

THE MEETING

A King with Aethelbert's standing in the Anglo-Saxon society would not have come to meet any stranger who presented himself at one of his ports. Without a doubt Augustine's Roman credentials, and the endorsement from Aethelbert's continental overlords, were an assurance that the meeting would take place and was the reason that Aethelbert allowed them such hospitality that his port offered.

The possible site of Location 2

Once the King had been alerted to the arrival of Augustine's company, he ordered that they should be given supplies. In offering hospitality Aethelbert asserted the traditions of both his Roman and Anglo-Saxon heritages, where the right to dispose of resources in food and shelter to guests arriving at the port that were his to command. With such a large group of men, he would very likely to have been accommodated at one of his central produce collecting and storage places, perhaps at one of his Royal Villas or possibly at the old fortress at Richborough, which was a strategically important defended stronghold and had held both the role of a defended centre and a central collecting place in the Roman period and where the great walls of the Saxon Shore fort remained and stand in the present day. If visitors to the port on such important business had to be accommodated in some form of guest hall, they may have been moved from the location fairly soon after arriving. However Bede's assertion that all the events took place on Thanet means we should look for a suitable location within the island. It is possible that the great Roman villa at Minster had served exactly the kind of temporary lodgement for travellers in the Roman period[1]. Accessible from the fleet from the navigable sections of the main Wantsum channel, the building had baths and other facilities that would allow the traveller to recover from a long journey before setting out again, along the ridge road, or by boat from Minster to the Roman road to Canterbury at Upstreet. While that building had undoubtedly fallen out of use by the late 3rd century, it is possible that landing stages and wharfs were still operated on the upper reaches of the fleet. The foundation of a nunnery on the site a century after Augustine landed, suggests that it may have been used in the past for a waterside trading centre with suitable halls and stores of supplies. It is possible that Minster, where one of Aethelbert's great halls may have succeeded the Roman building that once stood there, is the second location alluded to in Bede's account, we have no evidence yet that this was the case but the coincidence of requirements that supports this suggestion.

The meeting between Augustine and Aethelbert

Augustine's first meeting with Aethelbert was a formal diplomatic meeting between two parties who each had their own important roles, agendas and imperatives, an act of international diplomacy that would usher in the ideological foundations of the middle ages and moved the nation away from the classical past. How would a meeting between a rich and powerful King, whose power and authority might derive from a system which had direct continuity with the landed aristocracy of Roman Britain, and a representative of Bishop of Rome and head of the church in Western Europe be conducted? Each side would have to establish their credentials and assert their interest through the physical trappings that represented their authority and the symbolic forms of ritual drama that were part of their respective cultures.

Bede recounts that Aethelbert feared that Augustine wielded a supernatural power that would somehow exert a coercive influence on him, and therefore the king chose an open location for the two parties to come together[2]. In some ways the monks did bring a mysterious power that was a threat to the King. Aethelbert's submission to the authority of the Bishop of Rome would bring the Anglian Kings into the brotherhood of European monarchs who owed their spiritual allegiance to the church. Respectability among the monarchs of the west was linked to the association with the remains of Roman power and the contacts with the Byzantine Empire. However, acceptance of the Christian faith and with it the hierarchy of the Church and its own structures of power, might also undermine the traditional mystique of Kingship, one of the things *'so long observed with the whole English nation'*[3], that sustained Aethelbert's own power and authority. The Monks were brought to a Royal residence and they were given the considerable supplies of food and drink required by the large entourage. The hospitality was offered from the resources that were in his gift, from his own house, asserting his temporal power over the Monks.

The intention of Augustine's party was to bring the Angles into communion with the authority of Rome's church, and to persuade them to accept the Bishop of Rome as the spiritual patron of the English Kings and their people. Aethelbert was offered in return, the promise of eternal life and the acceptance and protection that the community would bring to his own position in the wider world. For the Pope in Rome, acceptance by the English Kings of his spiritual authority implied that, by that acting as the mediator between the King and God, he became the source of the King's own authority and legitimacy. Acceptance of the Church gave the Pope influence in a territory that represented the furthest reach of the power of Imperial Rome and rivalled the extent of the power of the dwindling Byzantine Empire with whose own religious patriarchs, he increasingly contended for spiritual power[4].

To understand where the meeting might have taken place, we need to look for somewhere within the cultural context of the Anglo-Saxon world. The story of the meeting recounted by Bede has the character of a formal assembly, similar to his later description of a later gathering of wise councillors held by Edwin of Northumbria to hear Paulinus preach[5], or the meeting that was held with representatives of the British Church, which Bede suggests took place by a great tree at the borders of Huiccii and Wessex, which was organised with the assistance of Aethelbert[6]. The open air element of the story perhaps reflects the traditional etiquette of the ancient assembly, where no one could get the upper hand by applying magical influence over a reasoned argument.

Bede said the meeting took place in the open air, which reflects the likelihood that Aethelbert would not have placed himself at a disadvantage in the negotiation by travelling to meet Augustine directly. Two large groups had to be accommodated in the location, and there was the possibility that a supernatural force would be unleashed. Although it seems that we have to discount any embellishments to the place, such as being held in the compass of a great tree which was suggested by Lewis without any known historical authority, we can expect that there was a traditional location for such a meeting[7]. Throughout the British Isles many moot-hills are recorded, where laws and judgements were given and debates between the key players in society were worked out. These mounds, also known as law hills and justice hills, a tradition from which our own parliament originated, were often located on prominent prehistoric burial mounds, partly because of their association with the ancient past[8]. The Anglo-Saxon people made use of prehistoric burial ground as a focus for their own cemeteries and there is evidence from the mound cemetery at Sutton Hoo and even at Stonehenge that judicial executions were carried out at these sites in the early Anglo-Saxon period[9]. It is likely that we should look for such a site in the landscape to place the first meeting between Augustine and Aethelbert.

If Augustine's group were accommodated at Cliffsend, they may not have needed to go far for their audience with Aethelbert and the assembly of his people. Among the graves archaeologists encountered on the hilltop at Cliffsend were several casual burials, placed face down in the soft sand of backfilled quarry pits[10]. Although it is not yet evident whether these victims are associated with the Bronze Age features, or Anglo-Saxon phases of the site, these may have been victims of judicial punishments enacted on a site with ceremonial significance which may have endured in the local culture becoming the site of Aethelbert's gathering place and a place of judgement. If Minster was the location where Augustine was given supplies while waiting for his audience, then there may be another clue to another possible location for the eventual assembly.

Various early chronicles relate the story of how Domneva (Domina Aebbe or Eormenburg) was given the land at Minster to found a religious community, the legend describes how a minister of the Kentish King Egbert (ruled 664 – 673), called Thunor (a variant of the Norse Thor), conspired with the King to murder Domneva's brothers in a succession dispute[12]. The legend tells that, in compensation, Domneva was given all the land her pet hind could run around in a single lap, which amounted to 80 sulungs of land on which she founded the double monastery at Minster. Incensed, Thunor chased the hind and was swallowed up in the earth, the site where this happened was covered with a cairn, which was subsequently known as *Thunores-hleaw*, (Thunor's Hill). This story may have been woven around the location of a moot hill, where a King might perhaps have been given bad advice by men who still adhered to pagan beliefs, which are personified in Thunor the minister.

The long ridge running east west across Thanet to the north of Minster is known to be the location of many Bronze Age burial mounds, represented in archaeological excavation only by their encompassing ring ditches, the ridge is also lined with cemeteries of the Anglo-Saxon period which have also been excavated by archaeologists[13]. On the ridge to the north east of Minster there is a high point at Prospect Hill where John Lewis reported the view was

> *'hardly exceeded in this Kingdom,.. we see not only this little island(Thanet)...but we have a view, at a distance, of the two spires at Reculver, the Isle of Shepway (Sheppey), the...mouth of the River Thames, the coast of Essex, the Swale, the British Channel, the cliffs of Calais...the town of Deal, the bay and town of Sandwich...the spires of Wodnesburg (Woodnesborough)...the ruines of the ancient castle of Richborough...the levels of Minster...with the river Stour running betwixt them...the fine and stately tower of the Cathedral of Christ Church, Canterbury and a compass of hills more than 100 miles in extent...'* [14]

Lewis noted that Thunor's Hill had traditionally been located near *Aldeland*, somewhere now in the vicinity of Alland Grange, Manston and probably beneath the western end of what is now Manston Airfield. Recent excavations on the chalk ridge at Minster have exposed several Bronze Age round barrows[15]. We do not know if there was a mound on the highest point, although some ring ditches were excavated when the airfield was extended in the Second World War which may have been associated with one that became known as Thunor's Hill[16]. What better location might there be for a King of Kent to meet and impress the representative of the Bishop of Rome with his temporal power than a site with such a prospect of his kingdom.

There is another intriguing association with the legend in that both Augustine and Mildred, a daughter of Domneva who came from France to take over as Abbess at Minster more than a century later, are reputed to have left their footprints on a square rock on landing in Thanet[17]. Mildred probably inherited the local tradition from Augustine, but a tradition of saintly footprints impressed in stone is common, particularly in Scotland where a well-known example is the footprints of St. Columba in Kintyre[18]. The saintly legends may have their origin in an earlier tradition where standing in the footprints impressed in a stone, often located in a moot hill, was a symbolic act when affirming oaths or crowning kings. The most famous example of a symbolic stone is the Stone of Scone, which was used most recently in the coronation of Queen Elizabeth II. Earlier still, Roman footprint stones were used to protect travellers before, and on return from, a journey, a tradition that persisted in Welsh legends. Pope Gregory had urged the early church to compromise with the existing pagan places of worship by adapting sites and festivals to Christian worship and it is possible that earlier traditions of oath taking and kingship, possibly of Pre-Saxon date, are veiled in this story[19].

Ultimately Bede records that, despite Aethelbert's desire to extend his hospitality to Augustine and his company, he was unable to abandon his belief in what he held in common with the Anglian people for an untested religion[20]. There appears to have been no uniform system of belief among the Anglo-Saxon people. The Franks and the Anglo-Saxons were unique among post Roman Germanic Kingdoms in having entered the Roman world as Pagans rather than as 'heretical' Arian Christians[21]. There were survivals from the beliefs of the pre-Roman inhabitants of Britain, those of the Romans and elements of the beliefs of the northern homelands of their ancestors. There were even Christians among them and Christians nearby in Scotland, Ireland and Gaul who had limited influences on their culture. The native British church was centred on the monks from Irish and Scottish monasteries, which had made no inroads into the conversion of the Angles, nor could they bring them to accept a form of Christianity that conformed to that practised in Rome[22].

Augustine was not the first Christian in Britain, but was the first to be sent explicitly to bring the unconverted population of Angles, and the existing Christians in Britain to orthodoxy with the Church of Rome. Augustine was to replace the ineffective effort of the Gaulish church to expand into Britain, challenge the existing Celtic Church to reform its practises and to extend the power of the Roman Church into a kingdom where pagan practises continued unchecked. By doing so the British

Isles entered into a process that would define European history for centuries to come.

APPENDIX 1 - EXTRACT FROM BEDE'S ECCLESIASTICAL HISTORY OF ENGLAND

Chap. XXV. How Augustine, coming into Britain, first preached in the Isle of Thanet to the King of Kent, and having obtained licence from him, went into Kent, in order to preach therein. [597 AD]

Augustine, thus strengthened by the encouragement of the blessed Father Gregory, returned to the work of the Word of God, with the servants of Christ who were with him, and arrived in Britain. The powerful Ethelbert was at that time king of Kent; he had extended his dominions as far as the boundary formed by the great river Humber, by which the Southern Saxons are divided from the Northern.

On the east of Kent is the large Isle of Thanet, containing, according to the English way of reckoning, 600 families, divided from the mainland by the river Wantsum, which is about three furlongs in breadth, and which can be crossed only in two places; for at both ends it runs into the sea. On this island landed the servant of the Lord, Augustine, and his companions, being, as is reported, nearly forty men. They had obtained, by order of the blessed Pope Gregory, interpreters of the nation of the Franks, and sending to Ethelbert, signified that they were come from Rome, and brought a joyful message, which most undoubtedly assured to those that hearkened to it everlasting joys in heaven, and a kingdom that would never end, with the living and true God.

The king hearing this, gave orders that they should stay in the island where they had landed, and be furnished with necessaries, till he should consider what to do with them. For he had before heard of the Christian religion, having a Christian wife of the royal family of the Franks, called Bertha; whom he had received from her parents, upon condition that she should be permitted to preserve inviolate the rites of her religion with the Bishop Liudhard, who was sent with her to support her in the faith.

Some days after, the king came into the island, and sitting in the open air, ordered Augustine and his companions to come and hold a conference with him. For he had taken precaution that they should not come to him in any house, lest, by so coming, according to an ancient superstition, if they practised any magical arts, they might impose upon him, and so get the better of him. But they came endued with Divine, not with magic power, bearing a silver cross for their banner, and the image of our Lord and Saviour painted on a board; and chanting litanies, they offered up their prayers to the Lord for the eternal salvation both of themselves and of those to whom and for whom they had come.

When they had sat down, in obedience to the king's commands, and preached to him and his attendants there present the Word of life, the king answered thus: 'Your words and promises are fair, but because they are new to us, and of uncertain import, I cannot consent to them so far as to forsake that which I have so long observed with the whole English nation. But because you are come from far as strangers into my kingdom, and, as I conceive, are desirous to impart to us those things which you believe to be true, and most beneficial, we desire not to harm you, but will give you favourable entertainment, and take care to supply you with all things necessary to your sustenance; nor do we forbid you to preach and gain as many as you can to your religion.'

Accordingly he gave them an abode in the city of Canterbury, which was the metropolis of all his dominions, and, as he had promised, besides supplying them with sustenance, did not refuse them liberty to preach. It is told that, as they drew near to the city, after their manner, with the holy cross, and the image of our sovereign Lord and King, Jesus Christ, they sang in concert this litany: 'We beseech thee, O Lord, for Thy great mercy, that Thy wrath and anger be turned away from this city, and from Thy holy house, for we have sinned. Hallelujah.'

NOTES

Introduction

1. Bing 1949, p.108 - 110
2. Stanley 1909
3. Mason 1897
4. Howarth, 1913
5. Mason 1897, Preface, vi
6. Sellar 1907
7. Mason 1897
8. Sellar 1907
9. Ibid, p.80

10. McKenny-Hughes 1897
11. Sellar 1907, p.80
12. Arnold, 1997, Chapter 1, p. 1-18
13. Stanley 1909, p.34
14. Mason 1897, p.281
15. Bing 1949, p.116
16. Arnold, 1997; Walton Rogers 2007
17. Moody 2008

Interpretations of the landing place

1. Sellar 1907
2. Gameson 1999, Hill 1990
3. Lebecq 1999, p.62
4. Mason 1897, p. 23-36
5. Stanley 1909, p.29
6. Bing 1949, p.114

7. McKenny-Hughes 1897, p.209
8. Dowker 1897
9. Moody 2008, p.144-145
10. McKenny-Hughes, p.233
11. Cunliffe 1968, p.224

Revisiting the landscape

1. McKenny-Hughes 1897, Dowker 1897
2. Osborne White 1928
3. Moody 2008, p.28, Fig.8; p.31 Fig.11
4. Sellar 1907, p.80
5. Moody 2008, p.140, Fig. 84
6. Roach-Smith 1851, p.54; Dowker 1897, p.131
7. Amos 2007
8. Gaffney et al. 2009
9. Moody 2008, p.46, Fig.16
10. Gaffney et al, p.30, Fig.1.12
11. Robinson and Cloet 1953

12. Grange 2006
13. Lewis 1736, p.47
14. Ibid, p.47
15. Met. Office 2013
16. Isle of Thanet Gazette, p.14
17. Isle of Thanet Gazette, p.14
18. British Library website
19. Delta Works website
20. Lewis 1736, p.200
21. Perkins 2006
22. Grange 2006

Reviewing the cultural context

1. Sellar 1907
2. Davis 1988
3. Ibid.
4. Sellar 1907,p.119-120
5. Jones and Mattingley 1990, p.176, Fig 5.23
6. Moody 2008, p.140, Fig.84 and Chapter 9
7. Ibid
8. Johnson 1979, p.23-33
9. Salway 1993, p.307-331
10. Cunliffe 1968, p.224-231
11. Ibid, p.237
12. Moody 2008, p.144, Fig.86; p.145
13. Peterson 1992, p.20
14. Anderson 1974
15. Moody 2008, p.52, Fig. 20
16. Lebecq 1999, p.50-54

17. Fleming 2011, p.30-60
18. Giles 1841, p.19
19. Fleming 2011
20. Walton Rogers 2007
21. Brooks and Harrington 2010, p.39
22. Sellar 1907, p.80
23. Fleming 2011, p.92-93
24. Thomas and Knox 2012
25. Davis 1988, Chapter 6
26. Moody 2008, p.168, Fig 100; Chapter 10
27. Brugmann 1997, Fleming 2011
28. Wood 1992
29. Care Evans 1986
30. Molas Website, Prittlewell Prince
31. Moody 2008, p. 140, Fig.84

74

The Landing

1. Sellar 1907, p.80-82
2. Carver 1998, Chapters 1 and 2; Carver 1992, p.41
3. Chadwick Hawkes 1969, p.191-2
4. Dowker 1897, p.142
5. Moody 2008
6. Lewis 1736, Volume 1, Frontispiece
7. Walton Rogers 2007, p.11
8. Wessex Archaeology 2006, p.11
9. Moody 2008, p.162, Fig.96
10. Andrews et al 2009, p. 199
11. Ibid

The Meeting

1. Moody 2008, p.155-156
2. Sellar 1907, p.81
3. Ibid, p.82
4. Mason 1897, p.173
5. Sellar 1907, p.156-158
6. Ibid, p.121; Mason 1897, p.130
7. Lewis 1736, p.117
8. Moot Hill
9. Carver 1998
10. Wessex Archaeology 2006, p.10
11. Carver, 1998, Chapter 6; p.137-144
12. Stevenson 1855, p.425-432
13. Moody 2008, p.94 Fig.45; p.161 Fig.95
14. Lewis 1736, p.120
15. Bennett, 2008
16. Grimes 1960
17. Stanley 1909, p.30
18. Petrosomatoglyph
19. Sellar 1907, p.103
20. Ibid, p.82
21. Davis 1988, p.103
22. Mason 1897, p.184-188

REFERENCES

Anderson. P. 1974. *Passages from Antiquity to Feudalism.* Verso. London.

Andrews. P. et al 2009. *Kentish Sites and Sites of Kent. A miscellany of four archaeological excavations.* Wessex Archaeology. Salisbury.

Arnold C. J. 1997. *An Archaeology of the Early Anglo-Saxon Kingdoms.* Second Edition, Routledge. London.

Bassett S. (ed.) 1989. *The Origins of Anglo-Saxon Kingdoms.* Leicester University Press. London

Bennet P. et al. 2008. *At the Great Crossroads. Prehistoric Roman and Medieval Discoveries on the Isle of Thanet 1994 -1995.* Canterbury Archaeological Trust. Canterbury.

Bing, H.F. 1949. St. Augustine of Canterbury and the Saxon Church in Kent. *Archaeologia Cantiana* 62, pp.108-29.

Brooks N. (ed.) 1984. *The Early History of the Church of Canterbury, Christ Church from 597 to 1066.* Leicester University Press. London and New York.

Brooks, S. 2007. *Economics and Social Change in Anglo-Saxon Kent AD 400-900. Landscapes Communities and Exchange.* BAR British Series 431, Archaeopress. Oxford.

Brookes, S. and Harrington S. 2010. *The Kingdom and People of Kent AD 400-1066. Their History and Archaeology.* The History Press. Stroud.

Brugmann, B. 1997. Britons, Angles, Saxons, Jutes and Franks. In K. Parfitt et al, *The Anglo-Saxon Cemetery on Mill Hill, Deal, Kent,* The Society for Medieval Archaeology Monograph Series. 14. Chapter 5.

Butler, R. 1999. *Richborough Port.* East Kent Maritime Trust. Ramsgate.

Butler, R. 1983. *Vital Haven.* The Museum of Maritime and Local History Deal. Ramsgate.

Campbell, J., John, E. and Wormald, P. 1991. *The Anglo-Saxons.* Penguin. London.

Care Evans, A. 1986. *The Sutton Hoo Ship Burial*. British Museum Publications. London.

Carver, M.O.H. (ed.) 1992. *The Age of Sutton Hoo*. Boydell Press. Woodbridge.

Carver, M.O.H. 1998. *Sutton Hoo. Burial Ground of Kings?* British Museum Press. London.

Chadwick Hawkes, S. 1969. Early Anglo-Saxon Kent. *The Archaeological Journal* Volume 126, pp. 186-192.

Chamberlain D. M. n.d. The Ancient Town and Port of Stonar. East Kent Maritime Trust/Thanet District Council

Cunliffe, B. (ed). 1968. Fifth report on the excavations of the Roman fort at Richborough, Kent. *Reports of the Research Committee of the Society of Antiquaries of London.* No. XXIII. Oxford.

Davis, R.H.C. 1988. *A History of Medieval Europe from Constantine to St. Louis (Second Edition).* Longman. London and New York

de la Bedoyere, G. 2006. *Roman Britain. A New History.* Thames and Hudson. London.

Dowker, G. 1897. On the Landing Place of St. Augustine. *Archaeologia Cantiana* Vol. XXII. p. 123-39.

Fleming, R. 2011. *Britain after Rome. The Fall and Rise 400 – 1070.* Penguin Books. London.

Gameson, R. (ed.) 1999. *St Augustine and the conversion of England.* Sutton Publishing. Stroud.

Gaffney, V., Fitch, S. and Smith, D. 2009. *Europe's Lost World. The rediscovery of Doggerland.* CBA Research Report 160.

Giles, J.A. 1841. *The works of Gildas and Nennius.* James Bohn. London. Google Books.

Grange, G. 2006. Double Tides in the Wantsum – Fact or Fiction. *Archaeologia Cantiana* CXXVI, p.381-390.

Grimes, W.F. 1960. *Excavations on Defence Sites 1939-45.* Volume 1. HMSO. London.

Howarth, H. H. 1913. *St. Augustine of Canterbury.*

Johnson, S. 1979. *The Roman Forts of the Saxon Shore (Second Edition).* Book Club Associates. London.

Jones, B. and Mattingley, D. 1990. *An Atlas of Roman Britain.* Guild Publishing. London.

Kirby, D.P. 1991. *The Earliest English Kings.* Routledge. London.

Lebecq, S. 1999. *England and the continent in the sixth and seventh centuries: the question of logistics.* In Gameson. R. (ed.) 1999 pp50-67.

Lewis, J. 1736. *The History and Antiquities, as well Ecclesiatical as Civil, of the Isle of Tenet, in Kent.* 2nd ed., reprinted in three volumes 2005. Michael's Bookshop, Ramsgate.

Mason, A.J. 1897. *The Mission of St. Augustine to England According to the Original Documents, being a Handbook for the Thirteenth Centenary.* Cambridge University Press. Cambridge.

Osborne White, H.J. 1928. *The Geology of the Country near Ramsgate and Dover.* H.M.S.O. London.

Perkins, D.R.J. 2006. Prehistoric Maritime Traffic in the Dover Strait and Wantsum: Some Thoughts as to the Vessels and Their Crews. *Archaeologia Cantiana* CXXVI. pp.279-293

Peterson, D. 1992. *The Roman Legions recreated in colour photographs.* Crowood Press. Wiltshire.

Robinson, A. H. W. and Cloet, R.L. 1953. Coastal Evolution in Sandwich Bay. *Proceedings of the Geologists Association* 64. Part 2.

Salway, P. 1993. *A History of Roman Britain.* Oxford University Press. Oxford.

Sawyer, P.H. 2002. *From Roman Britain to Norman England.* Routledge. London.

Smith, C.R. 1850. *The Antiquities of Richborough, Reculver and Lympne in Kent.* John Russell Smith. London.

Stanley, A.P. 1909. *Historical Memorials of Canterbury.* John Murray. London.

Stevenson, J. 1855. The Historical Works of Simeon of Durham. *The Church Historians of England, Volume III, Part II.* pp.425-432.
Archived at
GoogleBooks:http://books.google.co.uk/books?id=2_NLAAAAYAAJ&pr intsec=frontcover&dq=simeon+of+durham&hl=en&sa=X&ei=zzl9UZ3lK4 Kt0QXv4IHwDQ&ved=0CDAQ6AEwAA#v=onepage&q=simeon%20of %20durham&f=false

Sellar, A. M. 1907. *Bede's Ecclesiastical History of England, a revised translation with introduction, life, and notes.* George Bell and Sons. London. Text from Project Gutenburg:
http://www.gutenberg.org/files/38326/38326-h/38326-h.html#toc6.)

The Isle of Thanet Gazette 1953. *Photographs of Gale Damage in Thanet, February 1953 Reprinted from the Isle of Thanet Gazette 6th & 13th February 1953.* W.J. Parrett, Ltd. Margate and Sittingbourne.

Thomas, G. and Knox, A. 2012. A window on Christianisation: transformation at Anglo-Saxon Lyminge, Kent, England. *Antiquity* Volume 086, Issue 334, December 2012.
http://antiquity.ac.uk/projgall/thomas334/

Fleming, R. 2011. *Britain after Rome. The Fall and Rise 400 to 1070.* Penguin. London.

Hill, D. et al. 1990. Quentovic Defined in *Antiquity* Vol 64 No. 242 March 1990. pp. 51 – 58; http://www.archeurope.com/_texts/00075.pdf last accessed 28/03/13)

Vine, A. 2010. *In Defiance of Time. Antiquarian Writing in Early Modern England.* Oxford University Press. Oxford.

Walton Rogers, P. 2007. *Cloth and Clothing in Early Anglo-Saxon England.* CBA Research Report 145. Council for British Archaeology. York.

Wessex Archaeology. 2006. *Cliffsend Farm, Ramsgate, Kent. Archaeological Assesment Report.* Unpublished Wessex Archaeology Report.

Wood, I. 1992. Frankish Hegemony in England in Carver M.O.H. (ed.) *The Age of Sutton Hoo.* pp. 235-241.

Websites

Delta Works, All Saints Flood 1570. www.deltawerken.com/AllSaints-flood-(1570)/304.html
Last accessed 25/04/13

Meteorological Office 2013. Article on storm surges:
http://www.metoffice.gov.uk/education/teens/case-studies/floods
Last accessed 25/03/13

Amos, J. 2007. *Megaflood 'made Island Britain'.*
http://news.bbc.co.uk/1/hi/sci/tech/6904675.stm
Last accessed 25/03/13

Museum of London Prittlewell Prince:
http://www.museumoflondonarchaeology.org.uk/Services/PCaseStudies/UK-projects/Prittlewell-Prince/
Last accessed 26/04/13

Wikipedia Moot Hill: http://en.wikipedia.org/wiki/Moot_hill
Last accessed 6/04/13

Petrosomatoglyph: http://en.wikipedia.org/wiki/Petrosomatoglyph
Last accessed 6/04/13

British Library: *A Chart of the Isle of Thanet and Sandwich Marsh c.1548*
British Library, Online Gallery
http://www.bl.uk/onlinegallery/onlineex/unvbrit/a/001cotaugi00001u00054000.html (Last accessed 26/04/13)

Sources for Figure 6.1 and 6.2

http://www.newscientist.com/data/images/ns/cms/dn12289/dn12289-2_800.jpg

http://www.qpg.geog.cam.ac.uk/people/gibbard/

http://www.nature.com/nature/journal/v448/n7151/images/448259a-f1.2.jpg

INDEX

PLACES TO VISIT

St Augustine's Church and St. Augustine's Shrine

St Augustine's Church is a 19th century building, constructed of stone and flint by Augustus Welby Pugin between 1845-1852. Pugin moved to St Augustine's in 1843 following his conversion to Catholicism in 1835 specifically to be close to the spot where Augustine landed. The church was constructed next to his home 'The Grange', which was built in the same Gothic style. Today St. Augustine's is a local church of the Ramsgate and Minster Catholic parish and is an official shrine of St Augustine for pilgrimage. The church contains beautiful decoration throughout with stone and wood carvings, statues, stained glass and ornate tiles. For further information on the opening hours of the shrine and church telephone 01843 592071 or visit the website at http://augustineshrine.co.uk.

The shrine is located at:
Shrine of St Augustine (not postal)
St Augustine's Road
Ramsgate
CT11 9PA

The landscape of Augustine's arrival

A visit to the Church and St Augustine's shrine is an ideal starting place to explore the landscape of St Augustine's arrival in Thanet. From the church of St Augustine, head south west along St Augustine's Road to the Royal Esplanade and Government Acre where you can look out over the bay toward Sandwich, Richborough and Cliffsend and imagine Augustine coming ashore. A pleasant walk along the promenade toward Pegwell will take you on a route which continues through Pegwell village and along the cliff top paths to Cliffsend.

The Friends of St Augustine support the promotion of the church and assist with its restoration. For further information, visit their website at http://augustinefriends.co.uk/

St. Augustine's Church, Ramsgate